CW00919620

BRAND
MOMENTÛM

THE #**1** GROWTH METRIC FOR EVERY BOARDROOM

The science behind business growth and long-term success

How new thinking explains the forces
that shape consumer behaviour

TONY LEWIS

Copyright © Tony Lewis 2024. All rights reserved.

This book or any portion thereof may not be reproduced or used in any manner whatsoever without the express written permission of the publisher except for the use of brief quotations in a book review.

Strenuous attempts have been made to credit all copyrighted materials used in this book. All such materials and trademarks, which are referenced in this book, are the full property of their respective copyright owners. Every effort has been made to obtain copyright permission for material quoted in this book. Any omissions will be rectified in future editions.

Cover image by: Yesna99, 99Designs
Cartoons by: Gary Markstein
Book design by: SWATT Books Ltd

Printed in the United Kingdom
First Printing, 2024

ISBN: 978-1-0687405-0-3 (Paperback)
ISBN: 978-1-0687405-1-0 (Hardback)
ISBN: 978-1-0687405-2-7 (eBook)

Vision-X
20 Wenlock Road
London, UK
N1 7GU

tony@vision-x.co

Contents

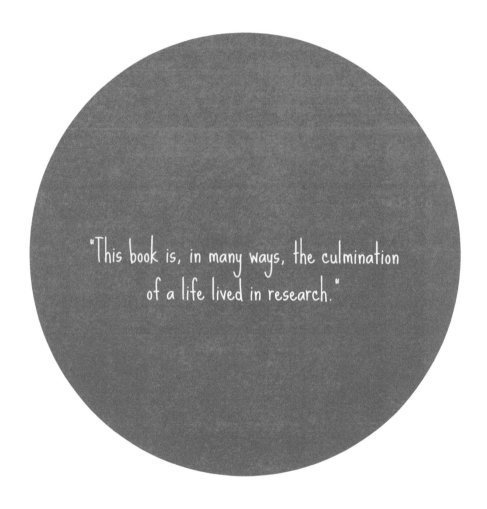

"This book is, in many ways, the culmination of a life lived in research."

Preface

Alex Brown

(Director of Insights, Vision One Research)

Many years ago, fresh out of university and eager to get my foot on the career ladder, I found myself staring vacantly at an Excel spreadsheet, trying and failing to make sense of all the tables, numbers and significance arrows that crowded the screen. I was working on my first project in my first junior research role. I thought I knew what our client wanted. I thought I had asked the right questions. But, confronted now with the results of my fieldwork, frankly, I was lost. There was no story. No strategy. To me, back then, it was just a lot of noise.

What was I thinking when I chose Research as a career path instead of taking a year off to backpack around Europe and misspend the last proper year of my youth?

As I was busy pulling my hair out, the office door swung open, and my new boss came barrelling through the room. We had yet to meet, but the place instantly lit up upon his arrival. Colleagues who hadn't so much as looked up from their computers all morning were now full of questions. It felt at that moment, that even the phones began to ring off the hook with potential new clients. There was a buzz in the air.

Tony Lewis introduced himself to me with a smile and a welcoming cup of take-out coffee. He sat down, and we spent the rest of the afternoon talking about research, exploring data, exchanging ideas, and figuring things out.

The 'figuring things out' has continued for nearly 15 years. From my career as a Research Executive to my current role as Director of Insights at Vision One, Tony and I have navigated the often challenging yet always fascinating waters of the Market Research world.

Since then, I have strived to bring that same infectious curiosity and desire for discovery to our work, clients, and team of talented colleagues, all of which gave me the research bug all those years ago.

This book is, in many ways, the culmination of a life lived in research. Throughout his career, understanding how to build and grow successful brands has led to many fruitful and long-lasting relationships with a diverse range of clients and businesses, from start-ups to huge multinational corporations.

Tony and the team at Vision One have worked for nearly 25 years across B2B and consumer sectors to deliver strategic frameworks that have become an essential part of any organisation's brand toolbox. Our BrandVision model is fast becoming one of the most powerful tracking tools available on the market.

Tony has worked across almost every sector imaginable, and in doing so, he learned that one thing connected them all: their pursuit of growth. But even more fascinating was their sheer lack of understanding of that growth journey – about momentum, how to measure it, and how to implement it within a business.

The strategies set out in this book provide business decision-makers with a clear, directive framework for measuring their organisations' momentum, understanding its impact, and, crucially, implementing a strategy for building momentum in every part of their business.

As you might expect from a Market Research professional, the book is grounded in robust insights from both primary and secondary sources. The examples used to illustrate strategies for increasing momentum are accessible, informative, and thought-provoking.

What is fascinating about the book is how it captures the simple but crucial idea of growth and interweaves it into the wider business mission. Tony demonstrates in this book how businesses can only achieve momentum when setting the conditions for it throughout the organisation, be that brand mission, proposition, advertising effectiveness, or strategy. Tony shows that momentum transcends all business levels and should be key in the decision-making process.

Brand Momentum is essential reading for anyone involved in a brand, which is to say, anyone and everyone in a business. For Marketers and C-suite in particular, a range of powerful tools are outlined to help in their understanding and implementation of a growth strategy.

Recognising the multifarious factors that influence a brand's perception, the idea that brands exist in the mind and are highly influenced by how we see them in a social context, all start to build a picture of the key factors determining a brand's momentum.

These culminate in the calculation and application of an organisation's Brand Velocity Score (BVS), a genuinely innovative measurement based on over 25 years of research and experience. The book successfully argues that any business looking to increase its momentum and grow should not only measure its BVS but also use it as a KPI to shape its current and future goals.

Tony and I recently met up in our new offices to discuss his plans for *Brand Momentum* and think about our plans for Vision One over the next year. The learnings about growth and momentum set out in this book are the foundations of our strategy, and we hope that through the continued monitoring and implementation of momentum, we will see the sustained growth the book talks about. We talked for hours, and I couldn't help but reflect that Tony still had the same enthusiasm, desire to discover, and visionary mindset that first gave me that research bug all those years ago.

It wouldn't be fair to say that this book is the end result of Tony's career in research because, knowing him as I do, he has plenty more up his sleeve. However, it is fair to say that when it comes to brand growth, he has figured things out.

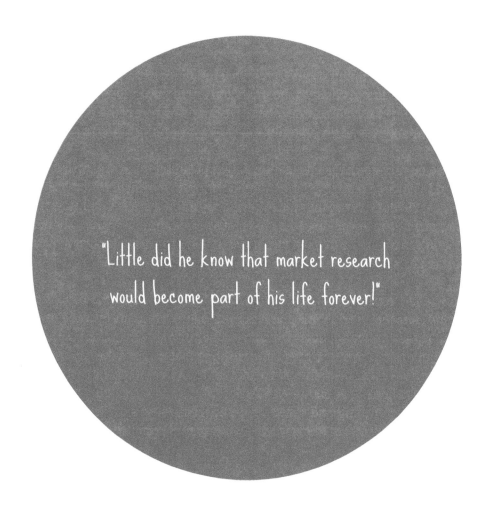

"Little did he know that market research would become part of his life forever!"

BRAND MOMENTUM: The #1 Growth Metric for Every Boardroom

About the Author

Tony Lewis was born on 12th July 1963 in Horsham, West Sussex, England. He is the son of Patricia and Philip Lewis and brother to his sister Shirley. He spent most of his childhood and early family years in leafy Sussex and Surrey before moving up to the Lake District (Cumbria), undoubtedly one of Britain's wettest places!

Today, he is the CEO and founder of Vision One, a multi-award-winning international research agency. The company recently celebrated its 25th anniversary since Tony started the venture in 1999. He is a Fellow of the Chartered Institute of Marketing and has been a long-term UK Market Research Society member.

Perhaps it was fate that Tony's mother worked part-time as a market researcher in halls and various locations across southeast England as a child. Indeed, he often sat quietly during the summer holidays, watching his mother interview people. Little did he know that market research would become part of his life forever!

His career started in the marketing department at Royal and Sun Alliance Insurance Group. Over a period of 15 years, he also worked at other high-profile blue-chip companies, including Lyons Tetley, First Choice Holidays and the Arcadia Group. As he says, starting up his own business was an act of madness, as he had no experience running a company, let alone any experience working in a research agency. But something inside felt like it was the right decision, and he must at least try to make it a success.

The consultancy soon took off, initially working for Marks and Spencer, Debenhams, the Arcadia Group, Sovereign Holidays and New Islington & Hackney Housing Association. Originally trading as 'Interface', Tony soon changed to a new name, 'Vision One', which was inspired by a few things, including the fact he was a big fan of the rock band Queen and their many hits throughout the 1970s and 80s, which included a song called 'One Vision'. In 2004, Vision One Research became a limited company with offices in Camden, London.

Winding forward to today, and with over 40 years working in marketing and research, Tony has become one of the most experienced researchers in the UK, having worked on over 500 brands of all shapes and sizes. Recent experience includes work for brands across many industries like Cancer Research UK, Coca-Cola, IKEA, Land Rover, Lego, Liberal Democrats, Lidl, L'Oreal, McDonalds, TUI, Unilever, Virgin and many more. He is a consumer psychologist, data analyst, and brand expert. He is skilled in most forms of research – qualitative, quantitative, neuro, behavioural and ethnographical. Essentially, whatever approach will get his clients the right insights!

This multidisciplinary research approach continues at Vision One. In 2023, the company took a step further by creating the Advanced Research Unit (ARU), tasked with tackling the most challenging insight problems – which remains his favourite hobby.

Tony and his son Jamie are in the process of creating The Brand Momentum Agency, a brand and marketing consultancy focusing on brand momentum and furthering the momentum story alongside Vision One.

Dedication

I dedicate this book to my wife Wendy, my son Jamie and our cat Mack*, who has sat beside me throughout the entirety of writing this book. I am eternally grateful for all their support, encouragement and inspiration, which have made this book possible and so enjoyable to write.

* Any typos you might find in this book are definitely Mack's fault – a result of stepping on this keyboard countless times in his attempt to gain some extra attention!

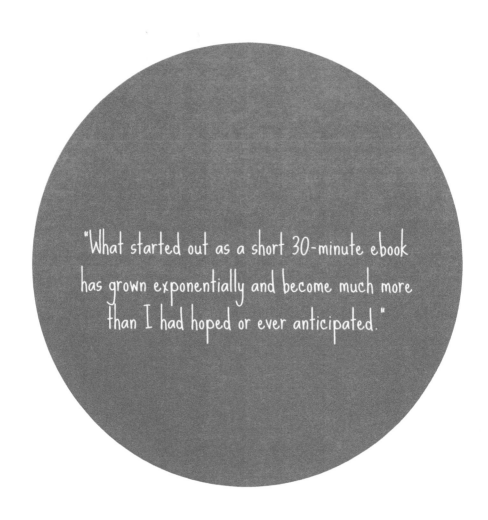

"What started out as a short 30-minute ebook has grown exponentially and become much more than I had hoped or ever anticipated."

Acknowledgements

The first person I must thank is my lifelong friend and wife, Wendy. She deserves special recognition for her continuous support, insightful ideas and unwavering belief in me throughout the year-long process of researching and writing this book. I'm also profoundly grateful to my son Jamie, whose arrival on May 12, 1995, changed my life for the better.

I extend my sincere gratitude to the team at Vision One. In particular, I thank Alex Brown, Kendra Furey, Dr Charlotte Baird and Adam Lunt for their encouragement and support of this project. The expertise and exceptional skills across the Vision One business have been invaluable in contributing to the research and ideas featured in this book.

I'm thankful to everyone who reviewed the early transcripts, offering their valuable thoughts, ideas, corrections and additional references. This includes: Susan Fermor, Anthony Harvison, Nigel Hollis, Richard Shotton, Mike Troy and Dan White.

Finally, thank you to the publishing team; Clare Robbin, Mark Beaumont-Thomas and Sam Pearce, along with Dan White, Jonny Moss and Gary Markstein who all played a crucial role in bringing the data and visuals to life.

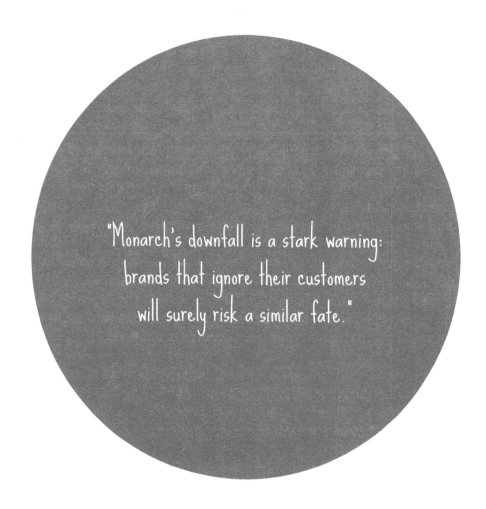

"Monarch's downfall is a stark warning: brands that ignore their customers will surely risk a similar fate."

Prologue:
The Discovery

Here's the origin story of many of the ideas in this book. A seemingly straightforward brand study led to an unexpected discovery.

In short, we uncovered an unexpected connection between brand dynamics and real-world outcomes when we undertook a project related to the airline industry, which happened to coincide with the demise of Monarch Airlines. This led to a deeper exploration of their demise and the lessons it provides boardrooms and brand owners across the globe.

So, the story behind this book started back in 2016, when I was working on an innovation project to create a more advanced brand image tracking system for Vision One's clients, which we later called BrandVision. The programme's focus was to provide a new measure of brand equity and to understand the forces that make brands attractive, and how these forces affect brand usage, loyalty and commitment.

We conducted numerous surveys and experiments, each aiming to test new ideas and provide normative benchmarks for launching this new brand tracking system. Each study focused on a different market, covering a wide range of brand metrics to ensure it was effective across business and consumer markets. Our research extended across entertainment, gaming, travel and leisure, digital and technology, grocery and packaged goods, financial services, retail, and distribution.

For no particular reason, it was focused on airlines on this occasion. While looking at the initial results, I recall noticing one standout finding that was slightly shocking: one of the brands in question had an extremely weak score. This blip was for Monarch Airlines. Essentially, we recorded a very low rating on a metric, which we later renamed the 'Brand Velocity Score'. Indeed, this score was the lowest we had seen in any of our trials. This result wasn't particularly action-worthy, but what followed was! Within months of this result, the news hit the headlines that Monarch had gone into administration. We were shocked and excited by this, not by the brand being in trouble, but rather that we had correctly identified this outcome simply through a survey and a realisation that we may have stumbled on a tool to predict the future!

About Monarch

Up until 2017, Monarch was the largest airline ever to have ceased trading in the UK, until the collapse of Thomas Cook a couple of years later in 2019. The claimed factors for Monarch's demise were various. Firstly, vicious competition and excess capacity on routes to southern Europe from other low-cost airlines. Secondly, travel fears resulting from terrorism in North Africa and thirdly, Brexit fears causing the depreciation of the pound sterling, which increased operating costs such as fuel, aircraft leasing and airport landing fees.

Why Monarch?

The brand was under significant pressure, but indeed, all UK airlines were subject to the same pressures. This then begged the question, "So what was different about Monarch?" The research we conducted suggested the airline's collapse was partly due to an inherent weakness in the brand image, specifically that it was suffering from low velocity and declining brand momentum. The parallel wasn't lost on us that a plane needs a critical level of momentum and velocity to stay in the air...

Monarch's downfall is a stark warning: brands that ignore their customers will surely risk a similar fate. Staying relevant means listening, adapting and always looking ahead. But there is hope; this story and just a single number proves the power of consumer insights to predict the future, giving brands the essential tools to control their destiny.

Winding forward to today, our understanding of brand momentum that predicted the demise of Monarch has grown significantly. The importance of understanding the direction and velocity of a brand has shown itself to be one of the most critical brand metrics. Current brand and marketing frameworks all position brands as stable, solid objects or phenomena which never change (unless things go wrong). These frameworks have disguised the fact that the most important driver of growth is change, in particular, what we refer to as 'brand velocity', which is the speed at which a brand is seen to be growing or declining.

BRAND MOMENTUM: The #1 Growth Metric for Every Boardroom

PART 1
DEFINING MOMENTUM

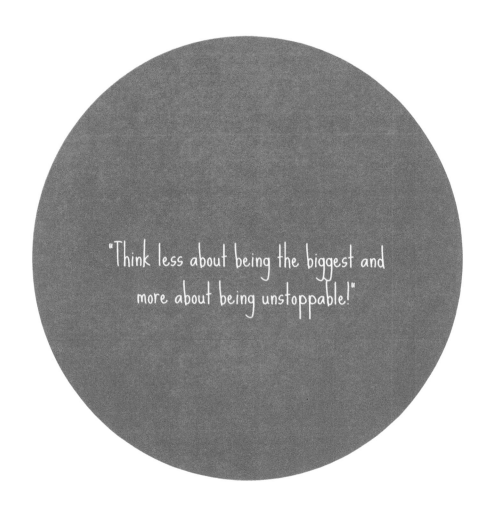

"Think less about being the biggest and more about being unstoppable!"

BRAND MOMENTUM: The #1 Growth Metric for Every Boardroom

Introduction
Why This Book?

I can teach you how to bewitch the mind and ensnare the senses. I can tell you how to bottle fame, brew glory, and even put a stopper in death.

J.K. Rowling, *Harry Potter and the Philosopher's Stone*

Over the last decade, the marketing world has become obsessed with performance or activation marketing. This obsession means that, in many organisations, the art of brand building has been lost. Start-ups and young brands often seem to believe the world revolves around social media platforms and immediate results. The good news now is that new insights are emerging, emphasising that brand marketing is more critical than performance marketing.

This book is for disruptors, game-changers and visionaries. It's essential reading for C-suite, marketers, and anyone interested in brand building and growing a business. It will show you new ways to grow and improve business sales, built on experience, science and research. It dispels a few myths along the way, too. It's also for market researchers and anyone involved in evaluating brands and brand tracking. The book focuses on helping you create a roadmap for brand health, more effective marketing, and long-term success.

Today, every business is bombarded with promises of how to achieve growth, and every CEO and marketing function appears obsessed with growth at all costs. I began counting the number of books on brand and business growth but soon gave up when I discovered there were over 10,000! Surprisingly, I couldn't find any books specifically about the factor which I believe is equally important, momentum, and how to measure it. There were only a couple taking a more generalised concept of momentum and applying it to business, life, and the stock market! So why are there so few books and authors exploring it? The intention with *Brand Momentum* is to plug this gap.

Chapter I

What is Brand Momentum?

While a good leader sustains momentum,
a great leader increases it.

John C. Maxwell

Brand momentum is the public's perception of a brand's performance and success. It measures the energy and influence of a brand on the customer and on its market.

Momentum combines two of the most powerful factors shaping brand perceptions: a brand's size and its velocity. Brand velocity is buyers' and users' perception of whether a brand is growing or not. Sustained brand momentum and sufficient velocity create a positive brand image, develop loyalty, and add value to a brand. They offer a glimpse into the future for many brands, and this predictive quality is unique to brand momentum theory.

Momentum is critical for growing and declining brands, both large and small, and is a must-have metric for all marketers and brand owners to use to measure success. It offers a simple-to-apply strategy and the secret to exponential brand growth.

So, to understand momentum, you need to track two things: how big your ship is (brand mass) and whether people think it's gaining speed or slowing down (brand velocity). Remember, bigger ships naturally lose a bit of speed the bigger they get. So, don't panic if your velocity drops slightly as your brand gains loyal customers. Focus on that overall momentum score!

Brand momentum is the hidden energy stored within your brand, the fuel that keeps it growing and thriving. To measure it, keep things simple. Track how many people use your brand and ask the most important question of all: "Do you think this brand is growing, declining, or staying the same?" This taps into the amazing intuition of the crowd, revealing how people perceive your brand's journey.

Mastering momentum and your velocity are the secrets to building a brand that lasts. Think less about being the biggest and more about being unstoppable!

One of the hardest challenges for Marketing Directors is striking the right balance between short-term gains and planning for long-term, sustained success. Achieving one-year or even quarterly sales targets is more often rewarded with bonuses than is 10-year-sustained brand momentum – that is just a harsh fact of boardroom survival. So, developing brand momentum is a far longer game but this book sets out to demonstrate that placing trust in long-term rewards is something all boardrooms should embrace.

So, this book is not about creating short-term wins. What word do you usually associate with 'momentum'? For me it's the word 'building' – building momentum. So, this book sets out a systematic approach to building long-term growth and health through a steady and cumulative process, preparing your brand and business for the battles ahead.

Brand Momentum and
the Laws of Physics

This book is a compilation of discoveries and insights I have accumulated over time, drawing inspiration from what at first sight might seem an unlikely source – the realm of physics and the ground-breaking work of Sir Isaac Newton. Newton presented his three laws of motion in the *Principia Mathematica Philosophiae Naturalis* in 1686. The intriguing parallels and analogies between brands and the laws of motion offer a unique perspective to explain consumer behaviour and how to achieve brand momentum.

In the realm of branding, the concept of momentum mirrors the fundamental principles of physics, offering a unique perspective on the behaviour and growth of brands. Just as objects in motion tend to stay in motion unless acted upon by an external force, brands that cultivate momentum are more likely to sustain their forward trajectory in the marketplace.

1. Consider Newton's first law of motion: an object will not alter its motion unless acted upon by a force. Similarly, brands that have built momentum through strategic positioning, effective marketing and strong consumer engagement are less susceptible to external disruptions and will keep going for longer.
2. Newton's second law, which states that the force on an object equals its mass multiplied by its acceleration, can be applied to brands as well. Brands with a higher mass or velocity will exert more influence or force on consumers and the market. This force will create greater attraction – helping brands grow and outpace the competition.
3. Newton's third law, often summarised as "for every action, there is an equal and opposite reaction," underscores the interconnectedness

of brands within the market ecosystem. Brands that exert a strong influence on consumers evoke reactions from competitors and stakeholders, shaping the competitive landscape and influencing market dynamics.

By understanding and leveraging the principles of momentum, brands can navigate the complexities of the modern marketplace with greater clarity and confidence. Like skilled physicists manipulating the forces of nature, marketers can harness the power of momentum to propel their brands toward success, shaping their trajectory and influencing their long-term growth and viability.

This book delves into how businesses create energy and momentum through their actions, especially in marketing and advertising. These activities are vital for boosting growth and building brand momentum. However, they face challenges from various sources, such as competition, societal trends, economic factors and political pressures. Understanding and overcoming these challenges is crucial. In the face of all the confusion from these opposing forces, it is critical to be able to measure your brand's performance and trajectory. To do so, we have created a useful and accurate measurement tool, the Brand Velocity Score (BVS). Unlike other metrics, the BVS has genuine predictive power. It's essential for marketers aiming for ongoing growth and longevity.

Core Beliefs Surrounding Brand Momentum

Brand Momentum introduces a new theory and approach to brand building, born out of evidence-based research, with predictive powers to signpost the future. It aims to give marketers a new way of thinking about brands that will help create new strategies to achieve longer-lasting success.

The ideas in this book are based on my first-hand experience working with brands, and brand tracking studies. However, it also borrows ideas from academia, other evidence-based research studies, and inspirations from hundreds of authors and researchers. It's also built on countless sleepless nights and twice as many café lattes to compensate!

This book is about the art and science of creating brand velocity and momentum. As you will see, it's a straightforward philosophy that is easy to apply and is measured by asking just one question to generate your Brand Velocity Score.

Using these metrics will enable you to see how the public perceives your brand, and give you a truer measurement beyond raw sales numbers as to whether it is growing or declining. It will quantify this with a straightforward, understandable score. This score reflects your brand's standing in consumers' minds. Tracking this regularly (e.g., annually, quarterly or more often) should run in parallel with the routine monitoring of your financial performance and other business indicators.

This single metric will not only help the direction of brands to be predicted, but it will also assist brands in reaching their maximum potential, growing faster, and, more importantly, lasting longer.

You may be familiar with an alternative brand image scoring method, the Net Promoter Score, as put forward by Fred Reichheld. His book *The Ultimate Question*, provides a measurement system and a blueprint for growth by focusing on loyalty and the degree to which customers recommend a brand. This book sets out an alternative brand image measurement system, to focus brand and marketing efforts by measuring brand momentum and building a strategy around that.

Brand momentum is based on three core ideas and beliefs:

1. **Brand momentum and the Brand Velocity Score (BVS) are the most important metrics for marketers.** And when fully understood, most other consumer brand metrics will pale into insignificance.
2. **Brands are in the mind.** They are mental constructs, and the best way to create strong brands starts by understanding the customer.
3. **Brands only succeed if built for the long term.** While short-term gains are significant, they are often tactical and should not be mistaken for long-term success. True, sustainable success is only reached by achieving lasting brand momentum.

Everybody is welcome to freely adopt brand momentum and the processes outlined in this book.

It's important to emphasise that this is just the beginning of my journey. While I have learned much about momentum in recent years, I acknowledge there is still a lot more to discover and questions still to answer. With many exciting projects in the pipeline, we're dedicated to the quest to uncover more about brand momentum, and how brand owners can use it to their advantage.

The Search for Momentum

Marketing and business leaders intuitively understand the universal appeal of momentum. Despite this strong interest, very few know how to measure it, and even fewer possess the knowledge to act on it.

Before writing this book, I had assumed that the momentum metric was well known and understood, but probably not by the majority. How wrong I was! While I have been unable to find any books about measuring or using momentum, I needed to find out whether it was currently being applied in the boardroom. So, we surveyed over 400 marketing leaders and CEOs to determine their awareness and usage of the metric.

Beyond establishing the critical importance of growth, our research explored whether CEOs and CMOs were aware of and interested in the momentum metric. If so, was it used to evaluate their brand marketing activities? Another area of interest was to see if momentum, or a similar metric, was being used by businesses to inform their strategies.

The findings clearly showed that only a tiny proportion used or prioritised momentum as a KPI. However, it was encouraging to see that the research discovered that nine out of ten business and marketing leaders were very interested in the concept; it also confirmed that leaders were in search of momentum. Clearly, there was a gap in the market for this book and that there was a need for the momentum story to be told.

The survey results and other conversations with business leaders revealed another startling fact: there was no consensus on which KPI was the most important. There were no clear standout metrics with broad appeal or widespread usage, and the most common metrics were related to customer satisfaction and brand awareness. However, a small group of CMOs, less than one in ten, prioritised a momentum-related metric as their main KPI – suggesting that a few are utilising this metric. Nonetheless, this also implies that this book faces a significant challenge, if my hopes of helping businesses discover and adopt momentum in every boardroom are to be realised.

To be honest, these results deflated me. I couldn't understand why so few companies used momentum or other growth metrics. Perhaps it was because those in the know were keeping it a secret? But this didn't make much sense. So, I was left with the notion that neither academia, marketing, nor business experts were aware of it, which would certainly explain why no one had written about it.

Given that virtually all businesses are focused on growth, don't you think the most natural question in the world could be to ask how consumers feel the brand is doing and whether they think it is growing or not? Surely, if a brand does its job, people will perceive it as evolving with a sense of direction, and purpose. Good examples are Virgin, Microsoft and Apple where they not only adapt but create new opportunities without compromising their core values or credibility.

We will revisit momentum and other metrics in more detail in Chapter IV, Measuring Brand Health. In the next chapter, we shall look at some of the ideas around how brands evolve throughout brand life stages, the importance of being first, brand mortality, and brand energy.

Marketers appear obsessed with brand reputation and image, and to such an extent, this focus is possibly to the detriment of brand growth. This focus on brand image could ultimately lead to a stagnant brand or even a tarnished marketing career if the brand doesn't perform. CMOs certainly have the tools to create growth, so if they are not going to lead the charge on growth – who is? The chances are it will fall to someone else – either the CEO or the Chief Strategy Officer (CSO).

The piece of the jigsaw that I believe many marketers are missing is the fact that increasing brand size and consumer perceptions of growth are the best way to improve brand reputation in the long term. One of the easiest ways to improve the brand image is simply to create brand velocity, and marketing has this at its fingertips.

Key Insight

The momentum paradox, in place today in so many companies, is that every business wants momentum, but very few seem to know how to measure or harness it. Understanding this metric is the key to unlocking sustainable growth.

Quick Definitions/Glossary

Included here are some mathematical equations, which may at first sight look complicated! In fact, as you will see in their use throughout this book, they are merely a shorthand way of describing some of the marketing principles around brand momentum.

Brand awareness (%) – Prompted awareness of a brand where consumers are presented with the brand name, typically within the market or category concerned.

Brand mass (m) – The number of users/buyers of a brand, i.e. the size of a brand.

Brand purpose – The reason for being for a company and its brands. This is often related to how the brand supports the wider world and tends to be more altruistic in nature.

Brand Velocity Score (BVS)* – The Brand Velocity on a scale of 0-100

Category entry points – The thoughts that buyers have as they transition into making a category purchase (e.g., Usage occasions).

Distinctive brand assets – Elements that can trigger the brand into memory for category buyers (excluding the brand name).

Impulse (i) – The change in momentum (i = mv2 – mv1).

IPA – The Institute of Practitioners in Advertising

Kinetic energy (e) – e ½ v2/m, i.e. the energy of a moving object.

---

* Brand Velocity Score and BVS are trademarks of Tony Lewis and Vision X

Mental availability – Mental availability is when the buyer notices, recognises or thinks of a brand when considering a purchase.

Momentum (p) – Mass times Velocity (m x v).

Net Promoter Score (NPS)[†] – Measure of the potential for word of mouth or 'Buzz' (NPS = promoters minus detractors).

User imagery – Perception of the target customer of a brand (who the brand is for).

Velocity (v) – The speed and direction of travel of an object.

WARC – World Advertising Research Centre

[†]   Net Promoter®, NPS®, are registered trademarks of Bain & Company, Inc., NICE Systems, Inc., and Fred Reichheld.

PART 2
GROWTH, BRANDS AND METRICS

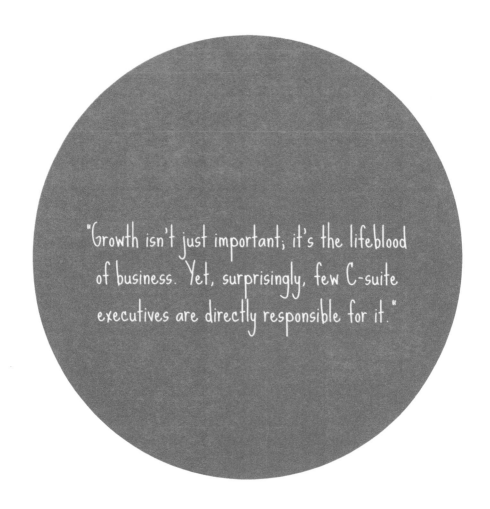

"Growth isn't just important; it's the lifeblood of business. Yet, surprisingly, few C-suite executives are directly responsible for it."

Introduction
Growth Matters

If you can't fly, then run. If you can't run, then walk.
And, if you can't walk, then crawl. But whatever
you do, you have to keep moving forward.

Martin Luther King Jr., minister, activist and civil rights leader

---

CEOs continue to prioritise the pursuit of growth. If you're not achieving your goals, perhaps it's time to change your metrics.

Growth is crucial for all businesses' long-term survival and success, enhancing business performance and profit. It helps to attract talent and investment and enables assets to be acquired, further boosting a company's value and prospects. Every CEO and brand owner aspires to achieve growth, yet for many it remains elusive. One stat I saw estimated that 25 percent of businesses have yet to experience growth in the past decade, with only around one in ten achieving a substantial annual growth rate of 10 percent or more. Many businesses have turned to short-term solutions in a scramble for growth in recent years, but research suggests that such short-termism harms business success – indicating that more focus on brand building is required.

A study among CEOs from medium and large businesses in the UK and the US explored their priorities and interests. The research survey by

Vision One confirmed the key priority for business leaders is growth. Technology (systems and IT) emerged as the second most crucial priority.

Numerous studies have confirmed that growth has been a consistent top priority for businesses. This was reflected in the 2023 Gartner *CEO and Senior Business Executive Survey*[1], which showed that CEOs and CFOs rank growth, technology (IT), and talent (people) as their top three priorities.

This begs the question: if growth is so important, why are there so few C-suite executives responsible for growth or with growth in their titles? The CRO (Chief Revenue Officer) and CSO (Chief Sales Officer) roles are often charged with ensuring targets are met - but not necessarily how long-term growth targets are achieved.

A LinkedIn search for 'Chief Growth Officer' yields less than 100,000 results. This might seem like a lot, but it's a drop in the ocean when you consider there are over 70 million businesses, that's only 1 in 700 companies having a CGO! Beyond CGOs, the most likely candidates in such a search are Chief Marketing Officers (CMOs), whose focus has traditionally been seen as driving growth. Indeed, many CGOs appear to have a background in marketing – perhaps suggesting that growth is a niche specialty within marketing.

In the business surveys we conducted, it was also fascinating to see that marketing leaders didn't quite agree with CEOs on their business priorities. Indeed, the research suggests that CMOs typically prioritise brand strategy, market research and brand image/reputation above growth or acquiring new customers. Indeed, it was rare for CMOs to put Growth as their number one priority, and this must surely create a disconnect between CMOs with CEOs and the rest of the C-suite.

So why isn't business growth at the forefront of CMOs' priorities? One simple answer might be that CMOs are simply being pulled in too many directions, having to juggle too many things. Their responsibilities often include; innovation (NPD), sustainability, pricing, customer relations, brand reputation, new technology etc. and trying to do this in the face of budgetary pressures. It's hardly surprising that their focus on growth can get lost in the day to day rigmarole.

After talking to several heads of marketing, I discovered that both metrics and objectives varied considerably from company to company, and marketers tend to prioritise their aims accordingly. Companies rarely seem to change their core metrics, so it may actually be the choice of these metrics which are to blame for the lack of focus on growth. Perhaps, if your brand isn't growing or performing, then now may be a good time to find a new metric that really focuses your organisation and marketing efforts on growth.

Whatever the answer, if marketers aren't prepared to champion growth, organisations should rethink the structure of the C-suite and ensure there is someone focused on it. Growth is a highly specialised discipline, and it's not the same as brand management, partnerships or sales development. The idea that everyone in the C-suite merely chips in, is destined to fail without someone driving growth as a priority. In my mind, the only way continuous growth is possible is if someone is directly responsible for it, and until someone is in place, then lacklustre results are inevitable.

Key Takeaway

Growth isn't just important; it's the lifeblood of business. Yet, surprisingly, few C-suite executives are directly responsible for it. CMOs often drive growth, but their priorities can clash with a CEO's, by prioritising brand reputation above growth. This disconnect reveals a potential blind spot in many organisations. So, where is the Chief Growth Officer? This begs the question: are companies structured to achieve their growth goals? The missing ingredient is often momentum, and in the following chapters we will show you how to add this crucial ingredient to your business.

Momentum: Uniting the C-suite

Chapter II

Brand Lifecycles and Growth Essentials

*It's only after you've stepped outside your comfort
zone that you begin to change, grow, and transform.*

Roy T. Bennett

**There are many analogies one can make between human life and
the life of a brand, yet far too often, marketers overlook the idea
that brands are mortal and start full of life. The most successful
brands evolve in size and shape over time, just like we grow
physically, mentally and emotionally through our lifetimes.**

Understanding a brand's dynamics and moving it out of its established
comfort zone are essential for growing and achieving success,
as these factors directly impact how customers perceive and react to
your brand.

While brand owners typically focus on growth phases, it's important to
recognise that all brands have a finite lifespan, often called a lifecycle.
The most commonly depicted brand lifecycle resembles a bell-shaped
path incorporating the S-curve, which illustrates a period of accelerated
customer acquisition during the growth phase.

Life Cycle: Four Basic Stages

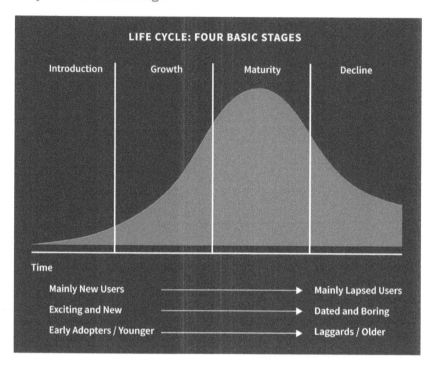

LIFE CYCLE: FOUR BASIC STAGES

| Introduction | Growth | Maturity | Decline |

Time

Mainly New Users → Mainly Lapsed Users

Exciting and New → Dated and Boring

Early Adopters / Younger → Laggards / Older

Contrary to this depiction of the bell-shaped curve, most brands don't decline as rapidly as they grow. Brands that experience sudden declines often do so for financial reasons, leading perhaps even to falling into administration. In reality, most brands experience a long tail or gradual decline. Stronger brands tend to retain more loyalists, which helps sustain the brand over time. Therefore, while growth is crucial, maintaining momentum beyond the growth phase is equally important for long-term survival. As mentioned earlier, the good news is that brand momentum is difficult to stop once it has been successfully started.

So, let's look at the four stages of the brand lifecycle in more detail.

a) Introduction Phase

The birth of a brand is an exhilarating time for most businesses and marketers, and getting off to a good start is essential. A huge amount of work will have been put into the brand launch, and this phase typically incurs substantial brand and marketing investment to grow distribution channels, as well as advertising and campaigns focused on making consumers aware of the product and its benefits.

This phase is relatively short in the life of a brand. It not only entails significant costs but also involves a substantial risk as the brand is exposed to competitors who are likely to react. In this infancy phase, brands are often small and insignificant and should focus on broadening their distribution and encouraging customers to try their product or service.

During or even before the introduction phase, brands should expect to face some rejection from certain quarters, especially if it is a disruptor challenging conventional wisdom – but if you have done your research, this should be nothing to worry about.

Brands and businesses often dismiss good ideas, based on flawed consumer research. In my early days as a researcher, Tetley Tea successfully launched round tea bags. Interestingly, their competitor, Brook Bond (PG Tips), had considered a similar concept but dismissed it after negative focus group feedback. Tetley's success came from offering samples for trial – participants discovered the round bag fitted perfectly in cups, creating a positive emotional connection. This underscores the importance of realistic testing: don't dismiss seemingly 'silly' ideas until consumers can experience them.

Rory Sutherland's *Alchemy* echoes this sentiment, arguing that market research can stifle innovation by placing too much emphasis on the majority view. True breakthroughs often come from catering for consumers with unique needs or perspectives – the 'weird' ones. As he says, '*The opposite of a good idea can also be a good idea*'. Brands should strive for bold differentiation from market leaders, offering something genuinely better (rationally, emotionally or physically).

Experience has taught me that easily replicated, overly familiar ideas rarely succeed. Pay attention to those concepts that mainstream buyers initially dismiss – they may hold surprising potential. As visual creatures, we're drawn to distinctive products. The most successful ones offer not only visual appeal but also practical benefits like ease, speed and convenience. To illustrate this, there is no better example than Liquid Death's launch into the stagnating bottled water market. At a time when everything looked the same, they took a fresh look and targeted a youthful music festival audience with a can that looked and felt like alchohol. Their stellar climb from £3m to £130m in three years shows what can be done.

Business textbooks often suggest that during the introduction phase, the primary focus should be on brand awareness. However, I believe it's more effective to concentrate on generating excitement and capturing consumer interest in your new brand. Our analysis of brands reveals that without stimulating interest or consideration, brand awareness provides little benefit for brands in most consumer markets, except in cases where competitor brands offer little differentiation – then the brand with greater awareness will win out. Moreover, evidence suggests that the fastest-growing brands excel at converting interest into purchases from new customers. Therefore, it's essential to emphasise brand distinctiveness and be clear about why people rationally or emotionally need your product, rather than solely attempting to raise awareness.

b) Growth Phase

The growth stage is characterised by growing demand, expansion, and the attempt to reach as many people as possible.

The growth rate will be shaped partly by the performance of your market/category, your brand, and your level of marketing investment. Achieving a competitive advantage at this stage is likely to be critical in attaining momentum. The faster a market grows, the quicker the brands within it will be seen to grow. This gives you a double boost and explains why exponential growth is possible. Conversely, if your market is static, then your growth will be stunted too.

During the growth phase, the brand will start to attract mainstream consumers who are looking to see what the excitement is about. It is likely that early resistance has now dissipated, and the brand should start to attract wider attention, build appeal, and create excitement. Brands in this phase often experience and benefit from increased visibility and increasing word of mouth as news spreads and the brand develops a following.

In his book *The Tipping Point*, Malcolm Gladwell aptly explains the brand lifecycle, emphasising that once an idea passes the tipping point, it spreads rapidly. Using Instagram as an example, Gladwell notes that while it initially experienced steady growth, around early 2012 there was a definitive moment when sufficient word of mouth made Instagram a global sensation, leading to unprecedented user growth and making it the fastest-growing social network of all time.

Momentum Makes Growth Easier to Achieve

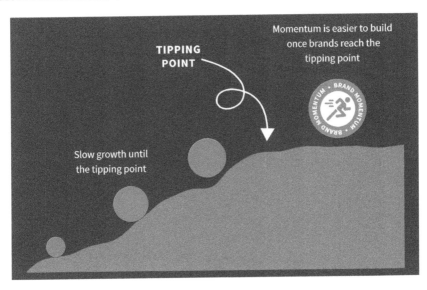

The Tipping Point suggests people are slow to adopt a product or a brand until social proof becomes evident. Similarly, people may quickly move on when the next big thing emerges.

Marketing efforts aim to increase interest during this period and reduce consumer resistance to adopting new technologies and products. However, our research suggests that these tipping points and S-curve patterns are relatively rare, primarily belonging to select B2C markets. Nonetheless, most brands can still achieve consistent growth, albeit with fluctuations influenced by various external and internal factors.

Even consumers acknowledge the influential role of word of mouth on their purchasing decisions, and trust other people's recommendations more than advertising. In most of our surveys, word of mouth is one of the top factors driving their decision – especially in new or growing brands. It should be no surprise to anyone that the world has seen phenomenal growth in influencer marketing over the past decade. Today, influencer opinions and recommendations via word of mouth or social networks play a significant role in spreading ideas, launching new products and delivering messages to consumers. We will revisit this later, but the ability to harness the power of word of mouth is integral to momentum.

Consider the case of Airbnb during its growth phase. Initially, it faced scepticism and resistance from traditional hospitality businesses and regulators. However, the negative reactions diminished as the platform gained traction and demonstrated its value proposition to travellers. Eventually, Airbnb became synonymous with unique travel experiences, appealing to a broad audience beyond its early adopters. People often share pride at having discovered and booked a gem on Airbnb, and the kudos (or social currency) from being well-informed and having a great lifestyle.

It's also worth remembering that competitors will not just be taking note but will be active and reacting to your initiatives – looking for ways to reduce the threat you pose or ride any wave you might be creating. Further investment will be required if you don't want to be swallowed up or overtaken by established players. Growth will depend on your ability to invest in the brand and adapt. This isn't rocket science, but how you do it might change once you understand momentum and how to achieve it.

As a rule of thumb, during the introduction phase, wisdom suggests you should focus on whatever manageable proportion of your target audience your budget allows. However, the focus should change during the growth phase, as growth will come from reaching more people (rather than loyalty). This will mean broadening your target audience and appealing to as many customers as possible. You may also have some additional product innovations (additional formats or variants) to help you stay ahead of the competition.

c) Maturity Phase

This phase represents a slowdown in the brand, which is often mirrored in the market and in other brands. Brands are often described as a leaky bucket that needs to attract new customers to replace any losses. During the maturity phase, brands tend to lose customers at the same rate as they attract new ones, and growth can be hard to sustain. There are many reasons for the slowdown; perhaps a brand has run out of ideas or possibly there is increased competition. Netflix is a good example of a brand entering the maturity phase. Despite being the market leader in a growing market, the brand has come under increased pressure from competitors in recent years and has lost market share.

Perceptions have shifted during this phase, from an exciting and new brand with dynamism to a brand that has matured. If it has performed well, it may be a significant player and benefit from its size and scale. Otherwise, it may just be in the doldrums and heading nowhere. This is a time to review and take stock. While sales and profits may still be healthy, the challenge is deciding where to take the brand next.

During this stage, brands can often have large budgets. Brand familiarity has probably been created over the years, but the brand may have fewer new stories to tell. Successful brands in this phase often move from rational advertising to more emotive messaging, such as ads which prompt fear, joy, sadness, belonging, humour and nostalgia. Such campaigns are proven to be effective, as we will explore later. These campaigns are designed to retain existing customers and attract old/ lapsed customers back to the brand. The brand needs to find other ways to grow, prolong its position and extend its lifecycle. Innovation can be useful at this stage, especially if the market is also showing signs of stagnation.

d) Decline Phase (Mortality)

This phase tends to unfold as a slow, drawn-out and often painful affair. Brand loyalists typically keep the brand alive, but without new customers, there is nothing to prevent the onset and continuation of decline. Rapid declines often occur when businesses go into liquidation, make a quick exit from the market, or face changes in legislation, among other factors.

Some of the reasons for this decline include:

1. **Changing social trends and values:** This typically encompasses trends such as health and well-being, cost of living, digitalisation, innovation and new technologies, which can impact any category or market.
2. **New and emerging competitive threats:** Where there is choice, there is always competition!
3. **The fickle nature of consumers:** People crave change in their lives, and they will rarely stick with the same brand forever, especially if their needs, values and lifestyles change.
4. **Weak brand or business management skills:** Most businesses fail because they make bad decisions along the way. However, many failed brands could have survived with good insights, knowledge and stewardship.
5. **Lack of money/investment and financial management:** Business pressure to deliver profits and dividends makes life harder for all brands.

During the maturity and decline phases, the holes in the leaky bucket appear to get bigger. A particular problem in this phase is the increased number of lapsed customers. Not only are lapsed users unlikely to provide any positive word of mouth, but they can be extremely hard to bring back. Successful brands keep the number of lapsed users to a minimum.

Achieving brand momentum in the decline phase becomes challenging, as investment tends to reduce while the brand is milked. The only way out of this phase is through a radical change in direction or a relaunch. Maintaining strong momentum levels will help ensure competitors are at greater risk and determine how long this phase will last. We will revisit this phase shortly as it provides important insights and lessons about momentum and what brand managers must avoid. Building on the idea of brand lifecycles, I believe three fundamental dynamics shape brand success and the life of a brand, which we will explore next.

Chapter III

Dynamics of Brand Growth – The 3 Fundamentals

A brand is the set of expectations, memories, stories and relationships that, taken together, account for a consumer's decision to choose one product or service over another.

Seth Godin

Let's face it: there are an infinite number of ways brands grow. Growth often comes from within a business through product innovation, diversification and brand extensions, but it can also be generated through advertising and marketing investment or even investment and acquisition.

The three most important rules, which I believe are crucial in understanding and building growth and momentum, are strongly linked to brand lifecycles, from humble beginnings and through the journey to growth.

1. The importance of being first (or very early) to market
2. The mortality of brands
3. The importance of an acquisition growth strategy

The Importance of Being First

*It's better to be first in the mind than
to be first in the marketplace.*

Al Ries

**Nothing is more important than being first in the
market – *especially* in the customer's mind. It's really
hard to dislodge brand leaders, and they often remain
the market leader for years, if not decades.**

Every brand is different, and every market is different, so there is no one-size-fits-all, but there are some basic rules of thumb that stand scrutiny and the test of time. History is littered with success stories for brands which entered a market or sector first (or very early), especially those which occupy customers' minds first. As it is sometimes known, the *First Mover Advantage* can make it much more difficult for others to follow. So, if you can't be the first in a market or sector, you should look to create a new category or find ways of breaking the rules within an established category. This is why most markets divide into more and more categories over time, as it can be easier to create a new category rather than topple the market leader.

Many familiar brands were first or very early to market and have since become global giants: Coca-Cola, McDonald's, Uber, Amazon, Kindle, eBay, Disney, Ford and Starbucks, to name a few.

However, the rule doesn't always hold. Technology and innovation can often change the rules – this explains why UK and North American businesses spend around £650bn a year on R&D. For instance, have you ever heard of Friendster? This was a social media platform before MySpace and long before Facebook – but it could not scale up in the same way that Facebook did. Sometimes, these failures appear not to succeed because they were simply ahead of their time or, more often, through a lack of investment/funding, which restricted their ability to compete.

One of the most devastating lessons I learned in my early days at Lyons Tetley was during the development of a new instant coffee brand that we were looking to launch. The company sought to exploit Lyons' brand name and its ground coffee heritage. Early-stage consumer research was extremely positive and indicated strong potential for the brand, so much so that a new factory and additional capacity had to be built to accommodate the predicted demand. However, by the time the factory was eventually built, Kenco, which also had ground coffee heritage, had managed to cement its position within the premium freeze-dried sector. So, when we tested the likely take-up of the new brand a couple of years later, the research, unfortunately, confirmed that the demand that was once there had disappeared, and the launch was canned. This lesson has haunted me throughout my career, and it's an essential lesson to everyone on the importance of speed to market and getting in first. Even today, I still wonder if the brand should have launched sooner without waiting for the extra capacity. I believe it would have been a different story!

In 1996, Gerard J. Tellis and Peter N. Golder, in their paper *First to Market, First to Fail? Real Causes of Enduring Market Leadership*, outlined their analysis of the PIMS (profit impact of market strategies) database. Their research highlighted that market shares across a wide section of businesses were around 30 percent for market pioneers, 19 percent for early followers and 13 percent for late entrants. This is good news and clearly supports the early mover advantage and its often-enduring benefits. However, something that caught my eye suggested another factor was at play and may have been overlooked by some. It is the idea that success can be built over time, which this extract summarises – giving hope to brands which are playing the long game:

> *"Many other markets came to be dominated by firms that persisted over many decades to finally establish the mass markets for their products. Kellogg, Hershey, Crisco, and Wrigley*

are household names, though their efforts in marketing and R&D are little known. In all these cases, persistence rather than order of entry or sudden breakthroughs was a key to success."[2]

Being the Best isn't Good Enough

Many brand owners mistakenly believe that if they can't be the first, they must be the best and that the best product will win. This notion is rarely true, as there is no such thing as a single, universal 'best' product in the customer's mind – it will be the one that suits each customer best. In most markets, premium and luxury brands tend to have smaller customer bases and smaller opportunities to grow, although their margins mean they can be very profitable.

Unlike 'maximising', where we look for the optimal solution (e.g., buying the best), 'satisficing', a combination of *satisfy* and *suffice,* was introduced by Herbert A. Simon in 1956. It is the idea that people don't always look for the best but simply something that does the job – a blend of satisfying and sufficing.

Satisficing

Satisficing is the decision-making process that occurs when there isn't sufficient information to make an informed decision. When we don't have accurate and meaningful information about which product is best, a brand can be used as a shortcut to help make the choice easier. For this reason, brands can be more successful in categories with fewer rational differences or where emotional decisions prevail.

Let's face it – we are an inherently lazy species, and our needs and values often focus on simplicity and convenience. We value speed, ease and low effort. We are always looking for better ways to make things easier and quicker, and it's for this reason that 'satisficing' exists. Whilst premium qualities can be crucial to some, especially in luxury markets such as fashion, cars, jewellery, etc, this tends to be the minority in most everyday markets except for the most discerning customers, where availability and buying to a budget are more important. Conveneince stores are a great example of when people choose to satisfice and select brands from very limited ranges.

You don't actually have to be the first, you just need to be the first in the mind of the customer. This battle for the mind is more important than physically being the first. In other words, you must be the first to take it to the mass market.

A common myth is that Henry Ford invented the automobile. The first car is actually attributed to Karl Benz in 1885/6 with a three-wheeled 'Motorwagen'[3]. Henry Ford launched his first car ten years later (1896) but created a new way to mass-produce cars, which helped him gain traction rapidly and so quickly established itself as first in the customer's mind.

We can't all be first to market; sometimes, it's far easier to learn from mistakes and improve on what is out there, and then attempt to steal a slice of the action. This is when it becomes important to differentiate your brand from the market leader or create a new category of your own to dominate. For example, take the yoghurt market, where there are now a dizzying number of categories: Organic, Probiotic Drinking, Greek, Indulgent, Kids, Skyr, Kefir... the list goes on. For each of these, I suspect different brand names will come to mind.

Ultimately, the only thing that matters is how the customer perceives the brand. Brands compete for the mind, which is why brand perceptions and positioning remain essential. Minimising the competition is important to becoming a long-lasting, successful brand. Putting the customer's mindset at the heart of your business is one of the most fundamental aspects of this book, as *Brand Momentum* is all about understanding the brand from the customer's perspective. The only way to find out where your brand stands and what it means is to talk to your target customers, listen to what they have to say, and, most importantly, ask the 'right' questions.

The Mortality of the Brand

The way a business brands itself is everything – it will ultimately decide whether a business survives.

Sir Richard Branson

Fear is one of our biggest motivations, and mortality is probably our biggest fear of all. Brands would be wise to remember their own mortality to help focus their attempts to grow and put a halt to their decline. Declining brands are seen as failures.

The concept of the brand lifecycle should be a part of every brand manager's toolkit. It's a sad fact, but all brands are mortal – they can't live forever. Looking at this more positively, mortality at least creates opportunities for others to launch new brands. Still, it also means every brand owner will need to plan ways to prolong the inevitable, using all the tools they have at their disposal.

In *The 22 Immutable Laws of Branding*, Al Ries and Laura Ries put forward Law 21, the concept of brand mortality. This states that all brands will eventually lose relevance, decline, or even disappear entirely. Brands must be nurtured, and they must adapt to change and the challenges of competition from both within and outside the category. By acknowledging change and the forces at play, brands can better prepare for the future, remain relevant, and achieve success.

Most brands tend to be associated with a specific product and market. Indeed, many brands not only represent but become synonymous with the category. Therefore, because of these strong associations, when a whole category starts to decline, so do the brands within it. Diversifying and moving a brand into new markets may stave off that decline. But, this can dilute a brand's distinctiveness, so beware – a brand is always most potent when it stands for one thing in the customer's mind.

It's impossible to properly understand brand growth without fully understanding decline. So, let's look at the brand lifecycle and brand mortality (aka the decline phase) in more detail before we focus on growth. Over 99% of the brands that have ever existed are now defunct. To be clear, I'm in the camp of researchers and brand owners who believe that brands are like people and have personalities. They each have their own life story, with challenges along the way; they build fans and followers, and ultimately, dictate their own lifespan.

Analysis suggests around half of new businesses never make it past five years in the UK and US, and only around 15% make it to 15 years or more[4]. It is also interesting to note that the average age of businesses on the S&P 500 has fallen from 61 years in 1958 to just 21 years in 2020. Business and brand lifecycles are often short, so let's explore the reasons for this and how decline can be postponed.

We shall see that the public has a collective view about brands and that these views and instincts can spell disaster for any company. Eliminating negative perceptions and behaviours, or at least minimising them, can help stave off the decline phase.

In another study by Vision One, exploring the perceptions by consumers of growing, static and declining brands, brands in the decline phase were distinctly different when compared to static or growing brands. The two most common negative image attributes for declining brands were:

1. Boring – The brand no longer resonated or had relevance to them.
2. Dated – The brand was seen as old-fashioned or no longer relevant to their needs.

Other factors associated with decline included: negative word of mouth or news stories (where negative stories outweigh positives); low marketing activity (probably due to lower investment and the negative outlook for the brand); poor brand health indicators such as shabby or outdated stores, over-persistent sales staff, low staff morale and poor customer service.

Brand decline, or a loss of relevance, causes a decline in brand momentum. Our experience shows that some brand tracking studies tend to focus only on the positive aspects of a brand, and ignore the less obvious opposing forces. We can see above how the negative impressions of 'boring' and 'dated' are correlated with declining brands. It also highlights recent research by Vision One in both the UK and the USA, that many consumers claim to be attracted to growing brands, and that even more (45%) claim to avoid brands they think are declining.

So, is it possible to escape from the decline phase? The inevitable slide from maturity to the decline phase is often slow, but the good news is that it can be predicted by the brand momentum measurement we will introduce later in this book. Encouragingly, there are many examples of declining and even defunct brands brought back to life. It's hard to believe that even Marvel, with its blockbuster movie franchises *The Avengers*, *Iron Man* and *X-Men*, filed for bankruptcy in 1997.

Generally, there are five key causes for this demise, and each may require a different solution. These are:

- **New innovations or competitors.** The arrival of a new player in the market can encourage consumers to reappraise their brand choices, and in some cases, this can leave existing brands looking old and tired. So, it's vitally important to keep an eye on the competition and assess what traction they are achieving, and most leaders will adopt a strategy to mitigate these threats.

- **Political, economic or social change.** There are always external threats on our doorsteps, including inflation, epidemics, international conflicts, etc. New legislation can also significantly impact markets, such as the UK sugar tax on soft drinks, which was introduced in 2018. However, the most common cause of decline is the changing consumer landscape and consumer lifestyles, trends and fashions.

- **Mortality is the natural ageing process of brands.** Neglect and a lack of cultivation or investment can also lead brands to age and fade away. Ski was once the dominant brand leader in the UK yoghurt market, but over time, a lack of investment and innovation led to its decline. Today, our research shows that although many people are still aware of the Ski brand, very few are purchasing it.

- **Brand sabotage.** This occurs when a company does something that damages the brand's reputation, whether deliberately or unintentionally. Product recalls are not just costly but significantly damage a brand's reputation. For example, in 2006, Dell recalled over four million batteries prompted by laptop fires, which appeared to be the start of 10 years of stagnation before returning to growth in 2018.

- **Loss of clarity and focus.** This can result in the brand losing its way. To keep up with a world where video games predominated in the late 1990s, LEGO overextended itself, but these developments were driving children away from LEGO. In 2003, the brand lost millions and was nearly brought to its knees by unbridled innovation, with too many people doing too many things to the brand. However, the brand recovered by streamlining its activities and adopting a more focused approach to innovation.

From a consumer perspective, friction has taken hold when brands are in the decline phase. The brand might be failing to attract customers, which it is unable to retain. Our experience of failed brands is that they tend to have a large number of lapsed customers. This means that there are generally only a few options for the brand in this situation. The first is to encourage lapsed users back to the brand by rediscovering something that they once loved about it. The second is to find a new audience or market for the brand (often a younger audience).

Sometimes, as markets mature, companies will face increased competition, which can lead to price wars, further reducing profits and the ability to sustain its brand. If you find yourself in one of these declining markets, you'll need to decide whether to cut and run or whether the brand has the potential to be reborn again. Unfortunately, not all brands are worth saving, and sometimes brands are not salvageable either.

"I'm afraid we've milked our products for all they're worth."

Adopting an Acquisition Strategy

Brands can enjoy higher loyalty, but only if they very substantially improve their penetration. A loyalty-first strategy is simply not a growth strategy. It is not possible to grow market share without reaching category buyers who never or very seldom buy your brand.

Byron Sharp

Acquiring new customers seems like the most obvious way to grow – but the reality is most marketers don't. It's time to rethink your brand strategy and start prioritising new customers.

I am a big fan of the work of Byron Sharp and his colleagues at the Ehrenberg-Bass Institute at the University of South Australia, built on the research by Ehrenberg and Goodhart. Sharp's book, *How Brands Grow: What Marketers Don't Know*, is informed by evidence-based marketing, focusing on what works in scientific practice rather than what should work in theory. The book argues the case for seven evidence-led rules for unlocking growth through brand marketing, but there is one that is particularly important in creating momentum.

While most of these rules are well established, I believe the most important and interesting rule is the first, which is that growth comes from focusing on acquisition and reaching new buyers. And this is precisely what you need if you want to create a momentum effect for your brand. It is based on evidence that growth comes mainly from attracting more customers rather than increasing purchase frequency or loyalty. This will often involve reaching less frequent and engaged category buyers, who may be less attentive to your advertising.

Another finding is that brand loyalty tends to increase in line with brand size – this is referred to as the *Double Jeopardy Law*. So, the rule suggests that not only do bigger brands have more customers, they also have more loyal customers. Essentially, it's very difficult, if not impossible, for small brands to gain many loyal customers, although membership and subscription models can help to address this in some instances.

As a brand grows, there will inevitably be fewer and fewer new customers to target. At some point, the brand will reach a saturation point, where it is difficult to attract any further customers. Growth then becomes a matter of expanding the category, entering new countries or international expansion. However, it's worth remembering that very few brands ever get this far, so don't get too concerned unless your brand is Amazon or Google!

Another important aspect of focusing on acquisition is that customers and market share gain will come from other brands in proportion to their size. So, the most significant gains will come from the most prominent brand. This is why it can be difficult to enter an existing market, as competing with the market leader (and its heritage and financial strength) will never be easy. In most cases, all brands must compete effectively with the market leader, who has many powerful attributes other brands cannot match – including size, reputation, history, momentum, etc.

Pull and Push your Brand

Growth can be achieved in one of two ways, although most brands will combine both to help balance short- and long-term sales. The first way, brand building and momentum, is essentially the subject of this book and relates to value creation. The second is Performance or Activation marketing, which focuses more on making an immediate sale. These methods are sometimes referred to as 'push vs pull' methods.

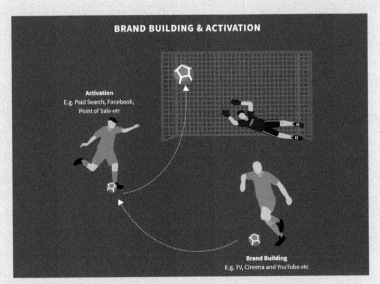

Thanks to Dan White of Smart Marketing for this idea.

Method 1 – Brand Building and Momentum (Pull)

The goal here is to attract people to the brand with a focus on brand building or value creation. Here, the emphasis is on increasing the number of people who want to buy your brand. It requires consumers to understand, need and want your brand. This approach is softer and more emotionally focused. This approach seeks to establish connections and provide value to the target audience. It often also seeks to create satisfaction, loyalty, and a willingness to pay the full price and even promote the brand to others.

Method 2 – Performance or Activation Marketing (Push)

The goal of push marketing is akin to getting a sale or purchase over the line. Many consumers are interested in trying products but often fall back on their default brand choice to avoid risk and simplify the decision, so marketing is needed to nudge potential buyers over the line. It often involves promotions, price cuts and persuasive marketing. It can be effective, but it is all short-term and rarely delivers long-term results. Indeed, research frequently shows that any sales achieved are unprofitable. The push approach can sometimes be effective for new brands that want immediate results and often involves direct and insistent language to coerce the customer. However, unless the product is outstanding, the chances of long-term success are remote, as when a competitor has a great offering you are unlikely to hold onto it.

Whilst both approaches drive growth, the emphasis of this book is clearly on brand building. However, it's hard to find a coherent theory about brand building from the perspective of creating people's perceptions. Most theories and experts tell you about the end-result i.e. that you need to be well-known and popular, have a good image and reputation, satisfied customers and have built loyalty, but they don't really explain how to get there. I believe momentum theory does this and provides a very clear path to achieving long-term success through a single metric.

Growth via Behavioural Science

To start understanding how to win more customers, we need a good understanding of the decision-making process. Most of us go through life happily unaware of a range of unseen forces that influence our behaviours and beliefs. As humans, our instinct to follow the herd is powerful (much as we might deny it to ourselves), and brands that understand this are more likely to grow. I refer to these positive forces as 'nudges' and any negative forces as 'sludges', ones that trigger poor decisions and ones not in the interests of the person concerned.

Behavioural science offers valuable insights into how we make thousands of decisions daily. It draws from psychology, ethnography, neuroscience and economics to understand decision-making, habits and behaviour change.

Behavioural biases and heuristics are mental shortcuts that influence our choices. I'll highlight some crucial ones for brand building and momentum. Great resources on the subject include *Nudge* by Richard Thaler, *The Choice Factory* by Richard Shotton, and Robert Cialdini's *Influence*.

Heuristics are mental shortcuts that can affect our decision-making and can play a part in helping brands grow. They are rules-of-thumb that reduce cognitive load and help making decisions much easier. They are often good when we need to make snap judgements such as when to cross the road, which washing powder to buy, what to cook for tea, who should I talk to in a crowd of people at a party. However, they can sometimes result in irrational or inaccurate conclusions or behaviours. Stereotyping is something we all do, and we use it in our judgements about people, and this extends to our perceptions of buyers of a given brand. This feeds into whether or not a brand aligns with our own self-image.

One of the finest (and earliest) examples of the importance of user imagery and projective techniques can be seen in the 'Shopping List' study by Mason Haire[5], which was reported in 1950 in the Journal of Marketing. Two shopping lists were prepared, which were virtually identical in all respects, except that one list specified *Nescafe instant coffee* and the other *Maxwell House drip coffee*. Respondents were split into two groups, each given one of the two shopping lists, and asked to project themselves into the situation as far as possible. They then wrote a brief description of the list creator's personality and character. The results were stark and showed that the group given the list with Nescafe Instant described the user as "lazy". The insights gave Nescafe a clear indication of the challenges it had to address. But the point here is that the insight was about the type of people who were thought to buy the product; simple things like age and gender are important when choosing the brands we buy, as we shall see later in PART 2: GROWTH, BRANDS AND METRICS.

Another well-known heuristic is scarcity. This refers to how we tend to value brands more when they are limited and can be used to the advantage of premium and luxury brands looking to increase sales. We are all competitive to some extent, and we measure our own success by comparing and contrasting with others. We've all heard of conspicuous consumption, and promoting limited time or limited availability significantly increases consumers' competitiveness and their intentions to buy.

Most nudges and biases are short-term and context-driven, tend to influence immediate decisions, and rarely last beyond the moment. This makes them ideal for advertising, promotions, and at the point of sale. They tend to encourage us to think or behave in a certain way. As such, they can be useful for kick-starting momentum, but I believe they are generally less potent for long-term brand building. Below, based on findings from other consumer research we have conducted over the years, I have outlined some of the biases that influence our perceptions and behaviours in the long term and, as such, relate to brand growth and obtaining momentum.

1. Herd Behaviour Biases

Unless you are a hermit, herd behaviour biases affect our daily lives. We value belonging and often follow the crowd to fit in, even if we pride ourselves on individuality.

Social proof is the idea that when people make a decision, they are influenced by what they think the common course of behaviour is. Many of us look to others to determine what the best course of action might be. In fact, drawing attention to the number of people using a brand is often more effective than highlighting its objective benefits. Witnessing others doing something can motivate us to follow suit – a powerful tool in advertising behaviour change. Look for adverts featuring many people doing the same thing to spot herd behaviour tactics. Coke's 'Holidays are Coming' ad (it's easy to find on YouTube) is a classic example – simple yet effective in evoking happy crowds eager for the arrival of Coca-Cola trucks.

Studies show we're not just guided by others, but we are also driven by fear of non-conformity and social pressure, and the more outer-directed we are, the more likely we are to feel this. This is why brand popularity and its standing in society are so important to the many choices we make.

We are now in an era where social media dominates everyday discourse and opinion-forming, and this could be said to be the ultimate herd-behaviour generator. Every brand is now subject to an avalanche of opinion via reviews, memes, 'influencers' and every viral technique out there. This is an opportunity, a threat and a challenge, depending on the current strength of your brand position, and largely beyond the scope of this book.

2. The Fluency Bias

Our brains prefer things that are easy to process and understand. This processing fluency can even influence how believable we find information.

Al Ries & Jack Trout's *The 22 Immutable Laws of Marketing* suggests a company can find immense success by owning a single word in a prospect's mind (think Volvo owning 'safety'). This distils the brand message, aiding recall and differentiation.

Jenni Romaniuk's *Building Distinctive Brand Assets* stresses the importance of branding elements that simplify decision-making. These learned associations, which include colours, logos, characters, shapes, slogans, etc., built over time, are powerful momentum tools. Research shows that brands with strong assets are significantly more likely to come to mind during the purchase process. This is why advertising and being seen frequently (e.g., by standing out) can be important in creating growth.

3. Expectation Bias

Our expectations powerfully shape how we experience things. This is akin to the placebo effect – belief fuels outcomes. Brands should aim to create positive expectations that drive adoption and loyalty. This is where advertising and crafting brand beliefs are pivotal. For example, the best way to convince someone that something will taste great is by showing people enjoying the food. Setting up these expectations and beliefs is a key part of advertising and fundamental to creating momentum. In general, advertising will set up beliefs about a product that will either be confirmed or refuted by the consumer the first time they try it. Successful brands will deliver on these beliefs, while those that don't will get rejected.

If you are interested in discovering more, Wikipedia lists over 200 nudges, biases and effects that you might find useful.[6]

Chapter IV
Measuring Brand Health

*Products are made in the factory, but
brands are made in the mind.*

Walter Landolf

How Brands Work

**Our understanding of brands is evolving. They are not just ways
to differentiate or authenticate, as signatures or hallmarks
do; they are powerful tools to help us make quicker and
better decisions. They don't just evoke powerful emotions;
they can even put us under a spell. Brands are, without a
doubt, the most powerful asset at a marketer's disposal.**

The concept of branding dates back to the Pyramids and Stonehenge. Artists from Mesopotamia, Rome, China and Greece used symbols and engravings to distinguish their work. Today, brands have evolved and can influence our feelings, thinking, and even our decisions and behaviours. They're not just slogans or images etched onto a product or pack; they're dynamic ideas within our minds.

Think of brands as mental concepts that exist at a conscious and subconscious level. From a neuromarketing perspective, brands are patterns of connectivity in consumers' brains – the sum of the emotions and experiences that create symbolic meaning. Studies have shown that the mere act of seeing the Coca-Cola logo can activate pleasure centres in the brain. This demonstrates the power of strong brand associations. These mental associations come from many places, such as online or in-store, from advertising to other people's recommendations. By measuring everyone's associations with a brand, we get a picture of the overall brand image. This is where market research is invaluable. Through surveys and talking to people, we can gauge the public's perceptions and memories, to develop a brand strategy and plan going forward.

When purchasing or making decisions, people are either consciously or subconsciously planning to satisfy their immediate or future needs and are buying that product or service in the belief they will make themselves (or their loved ones) happier. Neuroscience and those who study the brain suggest that powerful brands are deeply embedded in our memories and elicit feelings when exposed to them. Nike's *"Just Do It"* slogan evokes feelings of determination and empowerment. This emotional connection is a major driver of the brand's success.

Research confirms that most of our choices are influenced by our memories, experiences and emotions. Dopamine, sometimes cited as part of the 'pleasure system,' is responsible for our drive and decision-making, and is thought by some to be the most important as far as brand owners are concerned. In his book *The Branded Mind*, Eric Du Plessis suggests that marketers should focus on creating good memories, emotions and positive feelings – releasing as much dopamine as possible. We shall revisit emotions later in this book, as I believe these help to organise and dominate the mind as a whole and, therefore, are the most important decision-making factor of all.

Brands are multifaceted and have many features and benefits for both the brand owner and the customer. The three main ways they help us are:

1. Brands are promises that can alter our experience

Brands tell customers what to expect from their products and services, as mentioned earlier in Expectation Bias. This promise can be compelling. It has been known for a long time that brands can command a higher price, but they also impact how we think and feel and can even affect our performance. Many luxury brands, like Chanel or Gucci, promise exclusivity, quality and status. Even if the functional difference between their products and less expensive alternatives can appear small superficially, this promise commands a premium price.

Thus, strong brands can produce a brand placebo effect, in which their associative power can shape how we think, feel and act. In 2016, Frank Germann of the Department of Marketing at the University of Notre Dame's Mendoza College of Business found that if you can lead someone to believe the generic golf club they are using is a Nike, they'll drive the golf balls about 10% further.[7]

I also recall, whilst working for a fashion retailer, we found that customers often claimed to receive the best customer service at Marks & Spencer – but when we measured the service independently (via a mystery shopping study), we recorded no measurable differences with other leading fashion retailers. This led to the conclusion that the enhanced impressions of customer service at M&S were in people's minds rather than their actual experiences. This, for me, is a fundamental positive aspect of brands, as it can help people enjoy their lives more because of the added anticipation and heightened experiences they can provide.

2. Brands aid recognition and are shortcuts – so we don't have to think!

We come to recognise brands, and this creates a sense of familiarity. This 'recognition' is essential, as it helps minimise the sense of risk associated with trying or buying a brand. Think about the golden arches of McDonald's. They are instantly recognisable worldwide and offer travellers a sense of reassurance and consistency, wherever they are in the world. As we saw for the 'Fluency Bias', this makes the brand a go-to for reliable, quick and easy meals. Neuromarketing studies suggest that a brand can make someone feel more secure and increase serotonin in the brain, thereby assisting the purchase decision.

The idea of creating shortcuts is that making decisions requires energy and effort within the brain. The next time you go grocery shopping, look at how much time shoppers take to put items in their shopping trolleys. It can be less than a couple of seconds. Yet, how much do we know about the products we buy? For example, most of us have used Heinz tomato ketchup hundreds, if not thousands, of times, but how many of us know its ingredients? And where is it made? How is it different from other ketchups? Is it more sustainable than other ketchups? Does it contain more or less sugar? What is the price difference compared to an own-brand? You are likely to come up with the same answer as everyone else: *"I don't know"*, which applies to most of the products and services we buy. How often do you read the small print if you need further evidence? In truth, we are talking about emotions and subconscious processes when discussing brands. As consumers, we rarely care about the details – we use brands so we don't have to overthink our choices.

3. Brands differentiate, create preferences and help us make decisions

Strong brands help companies differentiate their offerings from competitors. Brands are no longer competing locally or nationally; they now compete globally, and as a result, branding has become even more critical in a world where we are all trying to gain attention.

Arousing curiosity is one thing, but it is essential to go further than this and ultimately win over people's choices. Brands create preferences, and these can, in turn, lead us to make irrational decisions – for example, buying a more expensive brand over another even if there is no perceived product difference or tangible benefit. The rivalry between Coca-Cola and Pepsi is legendary in the soft drink industry. Strong brand preferences are common among consumers and frequently start in childhood. Other influences include taste, advertising, and personal associations.

Many of us love brands; we not only buy them but also wear them, engage with them on social media, write about them, and even recommend them to others. These are examples of brands at their best. Many brand owners strive for badge value and create strong emotional bonds, ultimately leading to loyalty. Achieving high levels of affinity and loyalty often requires brands to align themselves with people's needs and values.

Why Metrics Matter

When it comes to evaluating brands and building plans, marketers need to find a way to measure their efforts. Brand metrics are the solution, as they take away the guesswork and provide a way to understand and communicate your goals objectively.

Metric (met.rik)
Noun
a number and measurement system that gives information about a particular process or activity

Think about the fitness tracker on your wrist. It measures simple metrics like steps and heart rate, but those numbers translate into insights about your activity levels and overall health. Similarly, brand metrics might seem simple, but they reveal crucial insights about your brand's health.

The role of most marketers is to communicate and to understand their market and their customers. They need to be able to answer questions such as who their customers are and what their motivations are. How do they make decisions? What messages do consumers respond to? Why do people prefer one brand over another? This is where the role of market research, surveys, metrics and measurements come to the fore and should be vital in the boardroom.

Metrics provide a way to objectively measure and analyse performance, helping businesses make informed decisions, track progress and identify areas for improvement. They are vital, as they signal priorities and clarify the end objective to everyone involved. They can also highlight the steps and processes that brand managers must take or consider to achieve these goals.

Today, dashboards, such as Microsoft's Power BI, are everywhere; these are a contemporary way to monitor your business and view all the metrics in one place, telling the story through visualisations. Think of it as an aircraft cockpit, where the pilot has all the figures and data they need to fly the plane safely. Brand management is very similar; brand owners require in-depth analysis and reporting to make decisions and manage their brand safely. The biggest challenge for any business is really knowing which metrics are the most important in securing success.

Benefits of developing and implementing brand metrics in your brand planning are numerous, but the five most important are:

1. **Performance Measurement**
   Metrics help measure the performance of the brand strategy and even the processes, campaigns and individuals involved. They provide a quantitative basis for evaluating how well your objectives are being met and can help identify areas that need improvement. Customer feedback, and understanding where a brand sits in the customer's mind, are integral to any brand's success. Many companies today use brand funnels to shape and measure performance. Netflix famously tracks numerous metrics, including how often viewers pause a show or abandon it altogether. These might seem like small actions, but they provide Netflix with valuable data on what content is truly engaging, influencing their programming decisions.

2. **Goal Alignment**
   As we have already seen, successful brands focus on growth and consequently track the relevant metrics to help achieve this growth across the company. However, for others, there are far too many metrics being used, which can only create confusion and cause conflict. We have already seen a classic example of misalignment, where the CMO does not share the CEO's primary goal of growth.

3. **Data-driven Decision-making**
   Many marketers these days are data-driven and rely on evidence to make decisions. Metrics are objective and reliable data for decision-making. Instead of relying on personal opinions, your choices can be based on concrete, measurable data, leading to more informed

and effective choices. This can help you make the process easier as it allows for a more rational approach to decision-making. In business, numbers often trump emotions. Spotify provides the music-tech industry with a wealth of insights by capturing data about a song's play time, what kind of device is streaming, and when it is played. Their 'fans first' initiative allows artists to identify and give their most dedicated fans access to special offers on concert tickets, gear, singles, and more.

4. **Risk Management and Planning**

Metrics enable brands to compare their performance against competitors, industry or category standards. In some recent in-depth interviews we conducted, we found that benchmarking was the number one goal for most brand tracking studies, as it helped to monitor trends and identify areas where improvements can be made to achieve a competitive advantage. Brand tracking allows for continuous monitoring of processes and systems, and when used correctly with the right measures, it can provide early indicators of potential issues or competitor movement. Having an early warning system like this will enable you to take corrective action before problems escalate. Imagine a new competitor launching a product with a disruptive advertising campaign. Consistent brand tracking could alert you to drops in your consumer awareness or shifts in consumer sentiment towards your brand or even a competitor. This allows you to analyse the situation and adjust your strategy, minimising any long-term impact.

5. **Accountability and Transparency**

Metrics create accountability for marketers by establishing clear expectations and providing a basis for evaluating the performance of their activities. They also contribute to transparency by providing a common language for communicating goals and reporting on performance in reaching these targets. They can also help ensure any investment and resources are allocated efficiently and appropriately.

Tracking Brand Health

Well-designed consumer surveys are the ideal way to understand a brand's meaning and assess its health. Most large businesses use brand tracking to measure their efforts, to determine if they are achieving their business and marketing objectives. Trackers provide insights into market and category trends, customer needs and perceptions, and overall brand health. This data is crucial for companies to evaluate goal achievement, make informed decisions, increase sales, manage competitive threats, and maximise returns on marketing investment.

When analysing brand image study results, compare them against your goals and ambitions, particularly identifying weaknesses or areas for improvement. While these aspirations are important for growth, remember that customer-focused brands are the most successful, long-term. Prioritise your understanding of what your customers want, need and value. Regular brand measurement, at least annually, is essential. This allows you to track key metrics over time, understand the drivers of improvement, and monitor competitor activity. Consider increasing measurement frequency to monthly for both short- and long-term impact assessment in fast-moving categories with frequent marketing campaigns or high competitor activity.

Keller's Brand Equity Model

When thinking about brands, Keller's Customer-Based Brand Equity (CBBE) Model provides a reliable and meaningful framework for understanding and measuring brands. It can be found in his popular textbook, *Strategic Brand Management: Building, Measuring, and Managing Brand Equity*, published in 1997. Think of the model as a ladder. New brands tend to start at the bottom (steps 1 and 2), adding more layers over time as familiarity and experience of the brand grows.

Larger, established brands compete at all four steps outlined below, as familiarity and experience increase. It's a good introduction to many of the important components of a brand and how people think and feel about brands.

Keller's Customer-based Brand Equity Pyramid

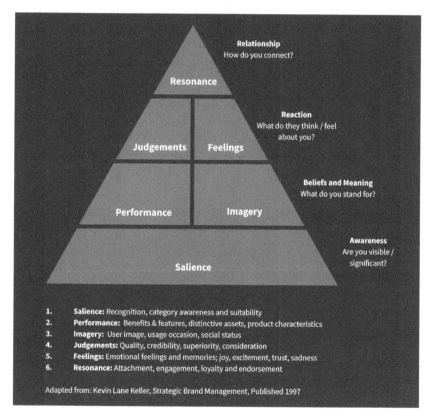

Step 1: Brand Salience (Are you noticed?)

This is the foundation of the brand equity pyramid. It defines how customers distinguish your brand from others. Brand identity is built during the introduction phase when consumers first take notice and seek to understand what the brand represents (category, appearance, function, differentiation). There's little relationship or trust at this level, and buyers focus on functional needs and benefits. Brand awareness and familiarity are common metrics, as being "top of mind" correlates strongly with purchase behaviour.

Brand awareness encompasses memories and experiences, including recognition of the brand identity (logo, slogans, colours, etc.), sometimes described today as Distinctive Brand Assets. The Mere-Exposure Effect[8], studied by Gustav Fechner and Robert Zajonc, demonstrates that increased exposure builds favourability. Visibility and availability benefit any brand. It was neatly described by Edward B. Titchener as the "glow of warmth" felt in the presence of something familiar.

Step 2: Brand Meaning (What are you?)

Once customers recognise your brand, they'll want to know more: Does it perform well? What are the benefits and features? Is it reliable and good value? Keller divides meaning into Brand Performance (qualities, popularity, advantages and promises) and Brand Imagery (brand story, usage situations, user imagery, and brand values).

Brand image metrics are crucial for evaluating brand purpose, proposition and positioning. Imagery also helps assess how well a brand delivers on growth fundamentals – relevance, innovation and leadership. People align themselves with brands that share their values, such as sustainability or brand purpose. Brand personality and archetypes are also relevant. Imagery can explore product perceptions or indirect impressions of the company through its actions and promotions.

Another perspective on imagery is Category Entry Points (CEPs),[9] a concept from Ehrenberg Bass. CEPs are rational and emotional reasons for choosing a category, similar to usage occasions, features and benefits.

User imagery is a crucial metric. It involves identifying the perceived target market of a brand (age, gender, life stage, businesses, etc.). This helps ensure the intended audience matches the actual customers who are buying or interested in buying the brand.

Food for Thought: The Power of Target Market

A recent Vision One study revealed intriguing insights into the relationship between the perceived buyer or user (i.e. user imagery) and brand health. Brands in decline exhibited substantially different user image age profiles than those brands seen as growing.

We focused on the perceived age of brand users. Remarkably, declining brands were seven times more likely to be associated with a user older than the respondent's age. Conversely, growing brands were consistently associated with a user younger than, or the same age as, the respondent. However, the research also suggests that brands can maintain the impression of growth even with an older image as long as the brand maintains relevance.

Step 3: Brand Reaction (What are their judgements and feelings?)

This typically emerges after consumers experience a brand. Negative experiences can damage a brand, while positive ones foster love, repeat purchases and recommendations.

Brand health surveys often delve into sentiment, affinity, brand love and relationship dynamics to gauge consumer feelings. We form relationships with more than just people; brands can evoke happiness and sadness, transform our sense of self, and influence how others perceive us. At their best, brands create powerful transformations and heighten our experiences. You don't need to look beyond brands like Apple to know that this is true for most people. But it's fair to say that most relationships are open and non-monogamous, so don't expect complete loyalty, as this is difficult to achieve unless you have a monopoly.

Metrics like empathy, satisfaction, loyalty, and Net Promoter Score (NPS - which reflects the likelihood to recommend a brand), all help to quantify different aspects of these relationships. We group these attributes due to their strong correlation, often measuring similar aspects, with the primary difference being the scales used. Analysis indicates that our measure of emotion stands out as the key driver of brand loyalty and NPS; after all, why would you recommend or be loyal to a brand if you didn't feel anything towards that brand? We will revisit emotions and experiences later in this book.

Step 4: Resonance (How deep is their love?)

When customers feel a deep connection with a brand – to the point of brand advocacy or loyalty – they've achieved brand resonance. If you use NPS, you would probably classify these individuals as 'Promoters.' Resonance indicates near-perfect alignment between a brand's various aspects and a consumer's rational and psychological needs and desires. This level is often experienced with luxury brands, where consumers willingly pay a healthy premium for this 'personal' connection.

Use Momentum-based Metrics!

If marketers had any clarity about how brands grow, surely we would see similarities in the metrics they use, but we don't! There's little consistency in how marketers tackle the problem of growth. Is this confusion a lack of knowledge or even a reliance on potluck?

In a recent business survey, we asked CMOs which key consumer metrics they measure and report upon. This enabled us to better understand what is important to marketers and get a window into their strategies and focus. We asked about their use of 15 metrics, and below are the seven that were most commonly seen as necessary for the Board.

Top Customer Metrics: Most Common Themes Used By CMOs.

MOST IMPORTANT METRICS (% RATING IMPORTANT)

- Brand Awareness
- Customer Satisfaction / Loyalty
- Brand Sentiment (Emotion)
- Brand Imagery
- Customer Lifetime Value
- Net Promoter Score
- Website & Social Media
- Conversion Rates (web/instore)

Sample: 300 CMOs across UK & USA   Source: Vision One: CMO Survey 2023

The findings were not what we had anticipated. The main conclusion was that CMOs were not prioritising the same metrics. Indeed, there was minimal, if any, consensus as to which metrics were most important. Very few picked the same three metrics, and each company had its own philosophy, measurements and priorities, rather than following a clear or common philosophy for growing a brand.

It was also interesting to see that the choice of metrics across the board appeared to be more focused on retaining existing customers (or concern about losing them!). This contradicts Byron Sharp's findings that brands grow through acquisition instead of focusing on existing customers. It also supports the notion that marketers are more focused on managing reputation and protecting customers, which might suggest they are also risk-averse. Budgets will restrict the growth prospects of any brand, and most marketers will have a constant battle to secure more funding for growth.

Fewer than one in ten CMOs prioritised a momentum-based metric as their main KPI, which suggests this book also has a big mountain to climb to share the message! However, even though the majority were not focused on momentum, a small number had it as their first or second most important metric. This indicated that a few believe quite strongly in the power of this metric.

One possible reason for the lack of use of consumer research in measuring momentum might be that there are more accessible, cheaper and reliable ways of measuring existing brand growth. Companies have their internal sales, profits and market share data. Why would you go to the time and trouble of asking a question in a survey when you already have all this accurate information at your fingertips? Well, whilst trends can be extrapolated from current data, none of it can accurately anticipate the future performance of a brand.

Direct consumer feedback via research aims to understand how consumers feel about something and what is going on in their minds. Many brand owners are not entirely in tune with their customers, and so research helps them to gain a fresh perspective and understanding of their audience to enable better decision-making.

Part 2 Round-up

Brands are powerful forces in our lives. They go far beyond logos and slogans; they create promises, act as mental shortcuts, and influence how we feel and think. To truly understand and manage a brand, we need metrics. These act as our brand's vital signs, guiding decision-making and tracking progress towards our goals. Market research helps us 'hear' the customer's voice, revealing our brand's image as it exists in their minds. Models like Keller's Brand Equity Model give us a framework to track this image and our journey towards ultimate brand resonance, where the customer feels a deep connection.

The fact that even top marketers disagree about the best metrics highlights the complexity of brand growth. It's a field where there's still much to learn and discover!

But overall, I'm left with a distinct feeling that many CMOs don't truly know what metrics they should be focusing on to grow their brand and reputation or which part of the brand funnel. As we shall see, finding a metric that can cover the top and bottom of the funnel and also instil growth would be the ideal solution. Welcome to brand momentum – the new metric for growth.

PART 3

UNDERSTANDING MOMENTUM

"Brand momentum is essentially the energy created by a business through its people, innovation and marketing. It's a force shaping a brand's future outlook and direction."

Introduction
Defining Momentum

Momentum is dynamic: Unless it is constantly nurtured, it will ebb away. However, the reward for that unstinting attention can be immense – it can make you number one in the world.

Jean-Claude Larreche

How is it that some brands achieve consistent growth and, in some cases, even exponential growth, whilst others remain static or even freefall into decline? Similarly, how come some brands last decades whilst others are gone in a flash?

As we shall see, momentum explains the above phenomena and not only enables young brands to grow but also helps big brands maintain their position. Ultimately, momentum is the life force of a brand. Learning what it is and how to harness it will help businesses maximise their potential. A dictionary definition of momentum might be as follows:

Momentum (Noun)
Pronunciation: mo·men·tum
Synonyms: Boost, Impetus, Stimulant, Motivation, Power, Force
Meaning: The ability to keep developing or growing
Equation: $p = mv$

The equation for momentum, p = m x v, relates to the physical world, where objects have a mass (size and weight) and velocity (speed and direction). Increasing either the velocity or the mass will create more force on impact. The bigger something is, and the more mass it has, the harder it is to stop. This is true in the world of brands and marketing, and the larger brand, or brand with more velocity, will be harder to stop too.

Very crudely, brand momentum is essentially the energy created by a business through its people, innovation and marketing. It's a force shaping a brand's future outlook and direction. Momentum uses the two most powerful elements in science, speed and mass, to explain it. Think of it as a rolling ball or, as I like to think of it, as a Zorb (one of those inflatable balls with a person in it where the Brand Manager is at the heart of it)!

The problem with brand momentum is that it has so many effects and facets it's very difficult to summarise, but I'll try with a few visuals below.

Visualising Brand Momentum

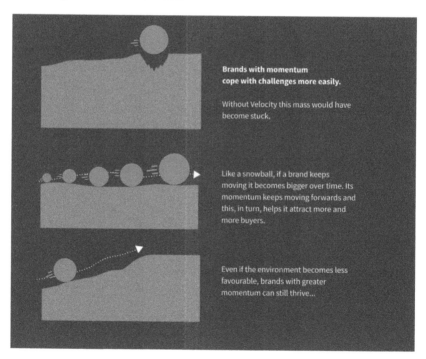

Brands with momentum
cope with challenges more easily.

Without Velocity this mass would have become stuck.

Like a snowball, if a brand keeps moving it becomes bigger over time. Its momentum keeps moving forwards and this, in turn, helps it attract more and more buyers.

Even if the environment becomes less favourable, brands with greater momentum can still thrive...

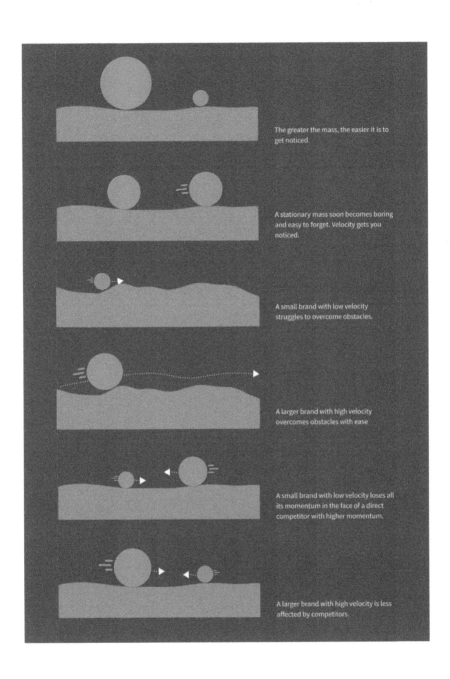

The greater the mass, the easier it is to get noticed.

A stationary mass soon becomes boring and easy to forget. Velocity gets you noticed.

A small brand with low velocity struggles to overcome obstacles.

A larger brand with high velocity overcomes obstacles with ease

A small brand with low velocity loses all its momentum in the face of a direct competitor with higher momentum.

A larger brand with high velocity is less affected by competitors.

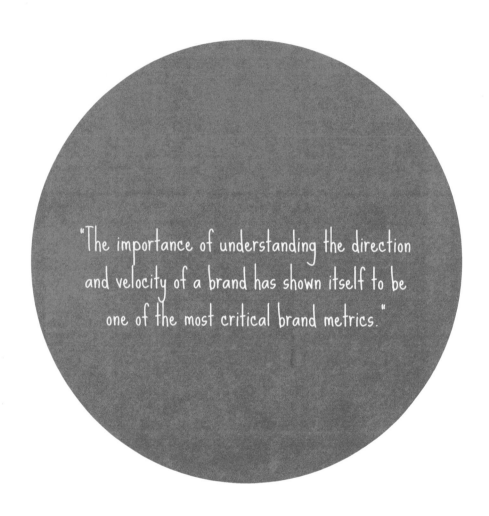

"The importance of understanding the direction and velocity of a brand has shown itself to be one of the most critical brand metrics."

Chapter V

A New Brand Measurement System

I think about myself as like an ocean liner that's been going full speed for a long distance, and the captain pulls the throttle back all the way to 'stop,' but the ship doesn't stop immediately, does it? It has its own momentum, and it keeps on going. I'm very flattered that people are still finding me useful.

Leonard Nimoy

Measuring Momentum

Big brands in motion are hard to stop, but so are smaller ones that are going even faster. Brand momentum captures brands in motion. It provides a new perspective on the battleground for brands seeking growth and prosperity.

Momentum is clear to see in the real world. Take a tennis player serving the ball or an opponent returning their serve. When two objects collide, the object with the most momentum wins – neither size nor velocity on its own is enough. In the same way, a brand needs both.

Sir Isaac Newton's physical laws of momentum offer important insights into how brands behave. In physics, momentum is given the symbol (p) and is essentially 'mass in motion'. The symbol comes from the Latin word impellere. 'Im-' as a prefix means inner, and 'Pellere' means to push forcefully. So, the word impellere means pushing with an inner source of energy.

As defined in this book, brand momentum is a very similar principle and uses the same calculation as mechanical momentum ($p = mv$). It is based upon the two following metrics.

1. Brand Mass (m) is simply the number of users. The more users (or mass) a brand has, the harder it will be for it to grow but also to slow down, and the larger a brand is, the more influence it will exert in a market.
2. Brand Velocity Score (BVS) is akin to velocity (v) and is based on a simple question: Is the brand growing, static or declining? It is essentially a measure of the speed and direction a brand is moving.

The calculation is expressed as:

Brand Momentum (p) = Brand Mass (m) x Brand Velocity (BVS)

The typical values for BVS range from 50 to 80, and the average for a category is usually around 55-60. Here are a couple of real-life examples of brand momentum scores, taken in 2023 from a representative sample:

Example 1 – Coca-Cola Vs Pepsi

Coke: 73(m) x 57(BVS) = Momentum = 4190
Pepsi: 63(m) x 54 (BVS) = Momentum = 3394

Note: Whilst neither brand has a particularly high velocity (Pepsi is lower than average), we can see Coke has a clear advantage, with a momentum score 25% higher than Pepsi.

Example 2 – Yahoo Vs Google

Google: 76(m) x 67(BVS) = Momentum = 5103
Yahoo: 29(m) x 30(BVS) = Momentum = 877

Note: Although Amazon has the highest score we have recorded to date, Google has one of the strongest brand momentum scores at 5103. Clearly, Google's momentum dominates Yahoo by a factor of 6. This helps explain why it dominates the search engines and makes it extremely difficult for Yahoo to get any traction when up against Google.

Measuring brand momentum is usually tackled and measured within brand health and brand tracking surveys. If you're running a medium-sized business, chances are you will conduct at least an annual brand health survey, whilst those who have larger marketing budgets tend to monitor their brand health more regularly (e.g., quarterly or monthly). As a rule, brand tracking once or twice a year is adequate for most consumer and B2B brands unless the market is young and evolving quickly (e.g. electric cars with new models arriving regularly).

During the lifecycle of any brand, the emphasis of the brand is to exploit its high momentum and grow its mass in the early years. Over time, the focus will shift towards maintaining its velocity in the latter years if it has reached its saturation point and there is little or no scope to increase its mass.

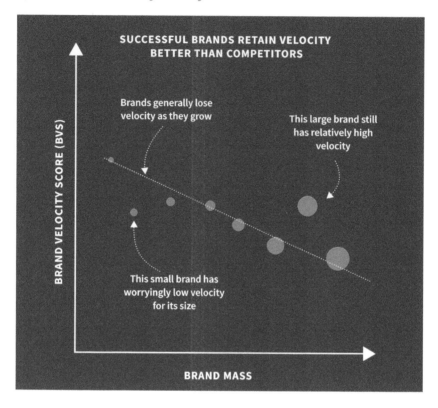

All brands inevitably start small, but with a successful launch strategy can soon achieve a high velocity. This will slowly reduce as time goes by and as the brand size increases. Smaller brands can manoeuvre very quickly, but the downside is that they can also be vulnerable to slowing down, so they require continuous investment to maintain momentum, just like any brand. The theory of momentum means that the size of the brand is as important as its velocity – so growing your brand size needs to be the ultimate goal, especially in the early years, to avoid being swallowed up or knocked off course.

On the other hand, large brands (high mass) with high momentum are like ocean tankers; the larger and faster they travel, the longer they take to stop. Supertankers typically take around 6-8 miles to come to a stop, and an emergency stop can take 1 or 2 miles. This idea of momentum is key, as it shows that the bigger the brand, the longer and harder it is to slow down. Therefore, a large brand with momentum will be difficult to beat. The good news is that big brands can still create brand velocity regardless of their age and size, and as we shall see later, momentum extends the life of a brand and can help avert the inevitable decline phase we covered earlier.

The best examples of brands maintaining or even growing their brand momentum are through large TV and advertising campaigns. Some of the most effective marketing last year in 2023 included Michelob Ultra (USA – Contract for Change), McDonald's (USA – Famous Orders), and Cadburys (UK – There's a glass and a half in everyone) – all of which tap into the powers of the momentum effect, as we shall discuss in the next chapter. All these ads are easy to find on YouTube using these descriptions.

In our tracking studies, we often see young growing brands gradually see their BVS fall - this is the natural decay all brands experience. The important thing here is for the brand to maintain a higher-than-average BVS if it doesn't wish to stagnate.

Another important phenomenon to be wary of, is brands that increase their mass in the short term, can see a small corresponding decline in BVS. This can occur as there is sometimes a slight delay between an increase in mass and an improvement in BVS. Monitoring will be required to ensure this decline in BVS isn't a long-term effect that requires attention.

This natural decline in BVS is another reason why it is important to measure the combination of mass (m) and BVS. As long as momentum is maintained, a declining velocity is not problematic. Essentially, as long as your brand momentum score (p) continues to grow, your brand health should be safe. The only thing to worry about is how the competitors are performing, as brands with low BVS will be the most vulnerable to competitor activities.

There is always some statistical noise and seasonal or competitor activity that can cause both mass and BVS to fluctuate. The important thing here is to monitor momentum, which is a much more stable metric and will provide a more reliable assessment of brand health over time.

Measuring Mass

A brand's strength and influence in a market are directly related to its size, and this has numerous advantages that smaller brands cannot match.

Measuring the size of your brand or your competitors' is a relatively straightforward process. In a nutshell, mass (m) is a measure of the number of buyers a brand has and is sometimes referred to as 'penetration' - the proportion of the target market who currently buys your brand. Penetration is the best way to assess brand size given it is a clear measure of the number of customers a brand has. Fortunately, it is also relatively simple to capture and measure accurately within a consumer survey. As you can appreciate, asking respondents to accurately guesstimate the frequency and quantity they buy of a brand is fraught with difficulties.

Measuring mass also means establishing whether someone has used or bought the brand within a certain period of time, typically a year. For example;

Which of the following brands have you bought in the last 12 months?

When posing this question and choosing who to ask, we recommend focusing on all category buyers and decision-makers as it will typically give a more accurate read on the competitive situation. Not only will current users be more representative of the market, but also, more importantly, they will be likely to have had exposure to the brands and have a greater appreciation of their marketing and business activities. Conversely, those with no knowledge or interest in the category are unlikely to harbour any meaningful current feelings, and possibly have outdated thinking and behaviours (e.g., buying brands that no longer exist). However, if in doubt or in a rapidly growing market, it is wise to cast the net wider and ensure you cover future potential customers.

Defining Your 'Current User' Timeframe

To identify your current users, we typically take the last 12 months as a good period to represent current brand buyers. However, you must select a reasonable period reflecting your specific market:

- Frequent purchases (weekly/fortnightly): Look at buyers within the last three months for a more accurate picture.
- Most other products: A 12-month window usually represents current buyers well.

The most important goal is getting an up-to-date snapshot of current behaviour – ideally representing the shortest time frame possible for your situation.

Getting the Right Sample

When seeking to get an accurate picture of your brand and the market as a whole, a representative sample of your target market is crucial. Keep these factors in mind, whether you're in B2B or B2C, when defining your sample:

- **Buyers or users?:** Be clear on the distinction between the two and decide if you should focus on buyers (more influential) or users (a wider demographic).
- **Include users and non-users:** Ensure you always reach beyond those who already use/buy and focus on the broadest target market possible.
- **Match market demographics:** Use external data to ensure your survey group has the right proportions of age, gender and other crucial characteristics found in your target audience. Also, think about who your competitors might be targeting and ensure they are included too.
- **Consider existing, lapsed and potential users:** Include all who might start using in the short or medium term. This is especially important if there is a long purchase process, such as buying a house or a new car.

Ensuring a matched sample for each wave is essential for reliable brand tracking; otherwise, differences between the waves may simply be due to fluctuations in the sample composition. This provides a reliable measurement and a fair basis for comparing your results against competitor brands.

When measuring velocity, we recommend only asking questions of people who are aware of your brand – and the same goes for competitor users. This will avoid recording complete guesswork and will ensure that respondents unfamiliar with your brand don't give misleading and inaccurate measurements. (Take note, sometimes people may not recognise your brand name but do recognise your logo or packaging, so ensure you understand how best to access whether they are aware of the brand).

You will need to consider the geographic composition of your sample. For example, if you are a national brand you should ensure the sample is spread across the country. Regional brands should clearly focus on the area and region of interest. However, if you have a niche brand, then initially you should focus on those who are most likely to experience the brand and its marketing.

Unlike traditional brand tracking, one of the great things about the brand momentum approach is that it is forward looking, and requires less focus on the past. As such, it doesn't require the same sample year in and year out – it can be adapted over the years to reflect a brand's changing goals and objectives. For example, a children's clothing brand might start out focusing on young mothers but then expand to all families and gifters for children.

Measuring Brand Velocity

Brand velocity fundamentally alters how we perceive brands. Understanding velocity is the energy behind the momentum equation and is crucial for achieving growth.

The Brand Velocity Score (*BVS*) is the cornerstone of the momentum equation, examining perceptions of growth (or decline). Yet, it receives scant attention in market research, marketing, or brand management literature. This may explain the inconsistent approaches within brand health studies. My research has even uncovered a US fast-food brand that dropped a similar metric from its tracker due to a lack of clarity on its purpose or actionable insights. Other brand owners have seemingly overlooked it for the same reasons. However, the potential business impact is undeniable once you grasp the BVS and its implications. You'll see how it shapes strategy, business, and brand planning, and even influences company culture due to its psychological element.

One velocity-measuring approach asks respondents to agree or disagree with: 'I think the best days of the brand are in front or behind them'. Another assesses intentions to 'buy shares in the company', gauging investment worthiness and deep-felt loyalty. In my view, neither question sufficiently captures growth or the rate of brand change. Understanding a healthy velocity is one thing; knowing how to create its perception is a brand marketer's dream.

Surprisingly, some of the world's strongest brands are among the oldest and most established, having successfully sustained their velocity. Before exploring this further, ask yourself: among Coke, McDonald's and Apple, which brand possesses the highest velocity?

You likely chose Apple... unless you are an Andriod user. But why? Apple's perceived momentum stems from relentless innovation – consistently updating core products (iPhone, iPad) while pioneering new categories (AirPods, Apple Watch). Their expertly crafted events and culture of secrecy fuel hype, solidifying their trendsetter image. Design aesthetics and exclusivity further bolster this perception. This much we know, but how do we quantify their velocity?

We can assess velocity through a single question about the brand in question or as an image grid for multiple brands:

- **Single evaluation:** Do you think brand X is growing, declining, or static?
- **For benchmarking:** Do you think the following brands are growing, declining, or static?

Notice the lack of a precise definition for 'growing'. This is intentional, allowing respondents to interpret it based on their individual understanding. While this introduces ambiguity, it's precisely where things get exciting; the metric encapsulates all the positive associations linked to growth, including success, popularity and more. Nevertheless, it is vitally important that the question captures any perceived changes in mass and the number of customers a brand has.

Tip for researchers: We have found that our simple three-option format (is the brand growing, declining, or static?) yields clearer and quicker answers than finer-grained scales. For example, the Likert 5-point scale (strongly agree, agree, neither, disagree, strongly disagree) and the Net Promoter 11-point scale (0,1,2,3... 10) tend to get people agonising about scoring correctly rather than focusing on the issue!

Importantly, brand velocity is comparative and best used for competitor benchmarking, so it needs to be assessed alongside key market rivals. Remember, brand momentum is heavily influenced by its specific market, which also has momentum. Your ultimate aim is to outpace competitors or the market average; otherwise, you will fall behind.

Unlike most survey questions focused on the individual respondent, the brand velocity question taps into broader social perceptions. This gives insight into societal trends and helps lessen the impact of personal biases.

Calculating the Brand Velocity Score (*BVS*)

While one could argue that assessing brand velocity by considering the proportion of people who perceive the brand as growing is reasonable, this approach has drawbacks. It leans towards an unbalanced perspective, neglecting the impact of negative sentiments on a brand's momentum (e.g., those who believe it's on the decline). A more comprehensive approach to measuring velocity involves subtracting the proportion of those perceiving decline from those perceiving growth.

BVS holds significance in Vision One's brand equity measurement system, BrandVision. This system is structured to ensure all metrics range from a maximum score of 100 to a minimum of 0. We assign weights to responses to meet this criterion, equating "Declining" with 0, "Static" with 1, and "Growing" with 2. This implies that if everyone perceives a brand as growing, the maximum score is 100, while if everyone believes it's declining, the minimum score is 0. Therefore, the fundamental Brand Velocity Score (*BVS*) is expressed as:

$$\text{BVS}® = ((\%\ \text{GROWING} \times 2) + \%\ \text{STATIC}) / 2$$

Following this calculation, if everyone views the brand as static, the score would be 50. Hence, any brand scoring below 50 is deemed as declining. In practical terms, after testing numerous brands, BVSs tend to fluctuate from as low as 40 to scores exceeding 75, with an average of around 58. For benchmarking purposes, we typically consider scores above 60 as favourable, indicating that brands are either growing or maintaining their market share and positioning.

In the next chapter, we will examine why momentum is so important and why it stands out as the metric of metrics. I do believe in the importance of challenging and scrutinising the momentum metric and philosophy. It must stand up to scrutiny if you are thinking about building your brand and business strategy upon it. For example, I would expect you to ask questions like the following:

- Does the question or metric reflect performance and growth?
- Can it be trusted and is there evidence to suppport it?
- Is it stable and measuring underlying long-term shifts?
- Is it predictive of growth or improved brand health?
- Does it work across different countries and cultures?
- Can businesses act upon this information?

In short, I believe the answer to all these questions is a big YES! So, let's look at some of these now.

An essential requirement for any brand-building metric should be capturing the essence of the underlying growth trend, i.e. long-term rather than short-term focus, such as immediate uplifts due to advertising that disappear quickly. Often, in brand tracking studies, during periods of heavy advertising, brands will experience uplifts in the number of buyers and other metrics such as brand awareness, consideration and empathy, including BVS. Whilst this movement and short-term uplift in metrics is desirable, the underlying (resting) levels of BVS are important. By monitoring BVS regularly over time, you are able to see a trendline emerging, which flattens out the distorting impact of promotional campaigns and seasonality etc.

Evaluating BVS across many markets and brands, we have seen that from one year to the next, BVS remains pretty consistent (with over 90% correlation year-on-year). This is good news, as, like most brand image metrics, it means these perceptions of growth and decline persist over time and don't fade quickly like the effects of advertising. So, if your brand has a high BVS, it's likely to retain it for a year or two rather than months! If it falls quickly, it's either because some activity has stopped or because there is a significant problem in converting this velocity into momentum. For example, the presence of a new competitor could change the landscape.

The even better news is that brand momentum ($p = m \times v$) is significantly more consistent as a way of measuring the underlying trend, and year-on-year shows a 93% correlation. In other words, brand momentum changes even less than BVS and is a more stable metric. This slow movement in the metric is one of the reasons we make it our recommended approach for measuring underlying brand health.

You may be surprised to hear that we often find that when brands grow their customer base (m) each year, they will steadily see their BVS fall – in other words, there is a negative relationship between change in brand size (m) and its velocity (*BVS*). This is to be expected due to Newton's first law of momentum, which states that momentum is conserved. So, as brands get bigger, their velocities will fall unless additional energy is applied. We define success more in terms of how long your brand grows or retains momentum, rather than on any short-term uplifts experienced. New brands must keep their newness, energy and excitement going for as long as possible – think years rather than weeks!

The importance of creating and maintaining momentum from the outset is why brands should invest heavily during their inception and growth phases. In effect, maximising the brand's BVS from the very start. This is good practice because of the inevitable fact that BVS will fall over time as the brand grows bigger. This high initial BVS at the beginning of the life of the brand will help attract new users and positive perceptions, whilst later in its lifecycle, retaining a reasonably high BVS will prevent competitors from making inroads and help prolong the brand's life.

But before laying down the reasons momentum ticks all the boxes for most brands, I have to share a story and insights about *The Code* – a programme that has transformed me as a researcher and opened my eyes to using research differently.

Welcome to The Code

Do you like guessing games? It might seem foolhardy to ask the public to guess things, but it can provide more insights than you might think. I'd argue it might even change the way you think about brands and market research!

When I look back to the time when we first developed BrandVision (our brand tracking system at Vision One), we tested a wide range of questions. I was sceptical about whether asking if a brand was growing or declining held any value. I clearly remember a loud voice in my head saying, *'Why are we asking a question that nobody knows the answer to?'*. Even employees in these companies won't have been told how the brand was performing, so how on earth could there be any real benefit in asking such a question to the broader public, with even less knowledge or interest?

Even today, one of the most common questions I get asked and challenged about momentum theory is, *"How will people know if the brand is growing or not?"* As we shall see, the answer lies in *The Code* – a mathematics-based BBC television documentary programme with Marcus du Sautoy which aired in 2011. This proved to be a pivotal concept that reshaped my perspective on market research and inspired new research methods.

What emerged from the programme was the idea that numbers can be seen in everything we see and do. What caught my attention, though, was a topic covering the 'The Wisdom of the Crowd' – the theory that crowds can guess or predict more accurately than any individual. Using a jar of jellybeans, Marcus asked 160 people to guess the number of beans. Amazingly, while individual guesses were wildly out, the collective result (average), as he predicted, was within 0.1% of the actual number. The example and its accuracy made me think about the implications for research and whether there might be some element of shared intuition at play. The programme is available on YouTube, do check it out, it's five minutes well spent. Just search 'BBC The Code The wisdom of the crowd'.

In truth, I was still unconvinced – it was TV, after all! So, a few years ago, we attempted to recreate my version of the trial at a major business exhibition we were sponsoring in London, where visitors could guess the number of jellybeans in our jar. Visitors were approached randomly and invited to participate, with the chance to win a prize for the closest guesses. Over the course of two days, we gathered as many guesses as we could, and amazingly, *The Code*'s prediction came true. Once again, to our delight, the closest guess was the average of all the guesses rather than any individual guess.

It has also been shown that groups are remarkably intelligent and often smarter than the smartest people. Findings from the TV show *Who Wants to Be a Millionaire* indicate that the 'Ask the Audience' lifeline is the best option available to contestants, giving 92% accuracy, compared with 'Phone a Friend', which only has 66% accuracy, with the '50:50' lifeline giving the worst option (i.e. 50%).

So, what does this have to do with research and brand momentum? Indeed, there is an argument that guessing the number of jellybeans is very different from trying to guess whether a brand is growing or not. People need some information about the subject; for example, if people were unaware of the jar and its size, then it would inevitably not have worked. However, we are conscious and able to express our views collectively for several reasons.

1. **We are attuned to what others do**

   We are highly social creatures; our human instinct means we gather information consciously and subconsciously about our world. In essence, we are programmed to learn from others through observation and word of mouth. Indeed, within the field of neuroscience, there has been a degree of speculation over the discovery of mirror neurons in the brain that respond to actions that we observe in others, ultimately helping us to learn from their actions. We all pick up clues about brands not just from advertising but increasingly from word of mouth and recommendations, product placement and sponsorships, social media, and even the number of people on the high street carrying branded bags and what we see in the shops. These clues all signal to society that the brand is popular and doing well.

2. **The brain is a prediction machine**

   We need a powerful brain to create judgements and ideas; fortunately, we have been given this gift. Malcolm Gladwell brings this concept to life in his best-selling book *Blink: The Power of Thinking Without Thinking*. The book and the central idea are based on our reliance on gut reactions and snap judgements (i.e. thin-slicing, as he calls it). He also makes the interesting point that most of the time, we're living on autopilot, and this autopilot means we typically learn by example and by the direct experience of what we see around us or how others act.

   I love Malcolm Gladwell's quote below. It makes the point that we are (subconsciously) aware of not only what's going on around us but also how we behave.

   > *"[Research] suggests that what we think of as free will is largely an illusion: much of the time, we are simply operating on automatic pilot, and the way we think and act – and how well we think and act on the spur of the moment – are a lot more susceptible to outside influences than we realise."*
   >
   > **Malcolm Gladwell, Blink: The Power of Thinking Without Thinking**

The Brand Velocity question does require each and every respondent to know, or at least hazard a guess, about the direction of travel of a brand (i.e. growing or declining). In effect, it is asking them to look forward into the future to make their judgement. The fact that we see the public often predicting changes in mass correctly, suggests that they are quite good at getting it right.

Here are some easy examples of times when we need to predict – it could be that you use memory to calculate it or simply use your gut reaction.

1. What letter comes next: a, b, c, d, e?
2. What number comes next: 1, 2, 4, 8, 16?
3. Complete this sentence: The cat and the __?

Hopefully, you found these reasonably easy and could calculate or estimate the answers (e.g., f, 32, and dog). The last one is more ambiguous and more associative, and we would probably expect the answer to be dog, mouse or fiddle. Whether or not you got it right isn't critical, but the fact that your brain was able to get close shows the power of your brain.

In sports, the brain always tries to assess what will happen next. Take golf, for example, which is one of my favourite pastimes. Before taking a shot, a golfer must assess the wind speed and direction, as well as the course conditions, and select which club they will use to reach the green. This will help them predict the likelihood of success. This advanced processing in the brain is handled by the anterior lateral prefrontal cortex at the front of our brain, and this will help the golfer decide their club selection, shot-making, strategy and tactics.

This predictive part of the brain is heavily involved in our decision-making and focused on estimating the chances of success. It explains why people find it relatively easy to gauge how they think a brand is faring and whether it is growing or not. But it also suggests that brands should focus their efforts on success and promising successful outcomes because this is what our brains look out for.

Further Evidence

Anything that won't sell, I don't want to invent. Its sale is proof of utility, and utility is success.

Thomas A. Edison

Throughout this book, I have demonstrated various theories and research findings, highlighting some of the important relationships and evidence we have discovered to date. This section provides a little more evidence from Vision One's Brand Bank and some of the work we have done to date.

The most important question really boils down to whether there is any evidence to indicate that BVS can grow (or reduce) mass. Secondly, related to this point, is there evidence that BVS can foretell the future, as I believe it did for Monarch?

About BrandBank

This chapter incorporates findings from Vision One's norms database, which we refer to as BrandBank. BrandBank contains information about hundreds of brands and thousands more brand measurements, allowing us to explore the relationships between brand metrics and customer behaviour across various categories and markets.

It incorporates all of Vision One's BrandVision metrics and other previously tested metrics currently being developed and refined regarding brand measurement and advertising effectiveness.

As previously discussed, momentum theory uses the 'Wisdom of Crowds' to determine whether a brand is growing or not. So, we can't analyse any individual behaviours to determine if the model holds. Nevertheless, we have seen evidence that people claim to be attracted to growing brands and avoid declining brands, which supports the magnetic qualities of BVS.

In the next chapter, I will also demonstrate that low brand velocity is associated with lapsed users while growing brands appear to retain current users. These findings highlight the fact that there is a behavioural aspect to BVS and that it is not just in the mind!

Many marketers and growth experts claim to prove their ideas by using correlations and regressions to explain their theories. I'm not a great believer in this approach because correlations cannot explain cause and effect; the same is true for regression. So, when you hear marketers claim to have run a 'Key driver analysis' to something, you should treat any such claims cautiously. In my experience, when dealing with the human mind, correlations tend to mirror associations in the mind rather than the drivers. As Mark Twain said, *"There are three kinds of lies: Lies, Damned Lies, and Statistics".* Don't get me wrong, statistics can be really useful to provide some extra insights, but they're only as good as the inputs that are used and the people who analyse them.

So, where does this leave us? The only reliable way to determine cause and effect is to look at a brand's metrics and predict what is expected to happen. Unfortunately, this isn't easy, as businesses will change and adapt to market conditions and competitor activities. For example, if a competitor starts advertising, it is common for a company to find ways to mitigate the threat. For example, a brand may react by advertising, running a promotion, innovating or copying the brand concerned. As we shall see, velocity (BVS) has both a short and long impact on the brand - the emphasis will depend on the activity being evaluated. For example, a price promotion might only have a short-term impact. Overall, we expect two general outcomes from the momentum theory:

1. Suppose all the brands in a market have a similar BVS. In that case, the theory assumes there will be no relative movement in any brand's size unless something significant happens to alter any particular brand's momentum. The good news is that, generally,

we find that most brands (or markets) do not see any substantial changes in their customer bases compared with the market overall. I refer to this as '*Happy Symbiosis*', which tends to happen when there isn't much marketing activity or investment in brand growth.

This happy stasis tends to be in less competitive markets. If your BVS is in line with everyone else, you shouldn't expect to see any change in the near or foreseeable future unless action is taken to improve your BVS.

2. On the other hand, for brands with a higher-than-average BVS, we expect to see brand mass (number of users) generally grow in the short and ideally long-term. Similarly, we should expect a decline in brand mass for low-velocity brands.

Impact of BVS on Change in Mass

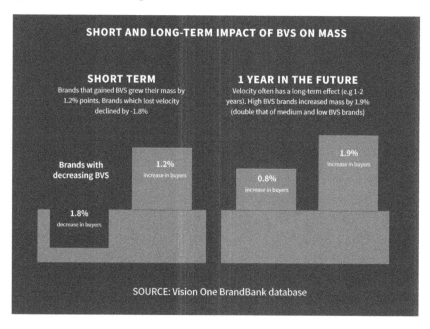

SHORT AND LONG-TERM IMPACT OF BVS ON MASS

SHORT TERM
Brands that gained BVS grew their mass by 1.2% points. Brands which lost velocity declined by -1.8%

1 YEAR IN THE FUTURE
Velocity often has a long-term effect (e.g 1-2 years). High BVS brands increased mass by 1.9% (double that of medium and low BVS brands)

Brands with decreasing BVS

1.2% increase in buyers

1.9% Increase in buyers

0.8% increase in buyers

1.8% decrease in buyers

SOURCE: Vision One BrandBank database

The left-hand side of the graphic above shows that brands which increased their BVS over the year also saw an increase in mass. Similarly, brands which saw their BVS fall lost 1.8% penetration (mass). Both these results are precisely what we would expect from brand momentum theory and highlight the ability of BVS to predict short-term growth.

The right-hand side graphic shows what happens a year after a high (or lower) BVS is recorded. In theory, we would expect to see high BVS brands outgrow others, and this is precisely what happens. This graphic shows that brands with a high BVS, gain 1.9% penetration a year into the future (i.e. twice the mass gained by lower BVS brands). This future gain in mass is what helps to prove that BVS actually drives growth, unlike many other metrics that fail this test. For example, brand awareness has no predictive power nor does it have any impact on your BVS.

Case Study 1 – Youth Employment

Whilst exploring brands in the arena of training and supporting youth employment, we discovered that Jobcentre Plus, a brand used by the Department for Work and Pensions to provide training, guidance and support, had a low brand velocity (BVS = 51) – well below all the other non-governmental brands we were tracking.

This was a poor position to be in, and we predicted at this time that things could get worse for Jobcentre Plus in the future. Our predictions came true, and over the next year, the % of users fell a year later from 6% to 4%. Somewhat unexpectedly, not only did mass drop, but we also found that prompted brand awareness also fell over this period. (Note: Typically, declines in brand awareness are generally very slow).

However, whilst Jobcentre Plus was struggling, two brands were leading the way in terms of attaining a strong BVS. These were Indeed (BVS = 69), a global employment website for job listings, widely used by the target market, and LinkedIn (BVS = 72), the world's largest business and employment social media platform. With their high BVSs, we predicted that there would be increases in the number of users (m). This proved to be the case, and both brands recorded significant gains in awareness, consideration and usage a year later.

Year-on-Year Changes in Awareness, Interest and Mass

	High Momentum LinkedIn BVS = 72	High Momentum Indeed BVS = 69	Low Momentum JobcentrePlus BVS = 51
Prompted Awareness	57 ▸ 64 y/y = +5	58 ▸ 67 y/y = +9	41 ▸ 39 y/y = -2
Interest	32 ▸ 41 y/y = +9	40 ▸ 49 y/y = +9	17 ▸ 15 y/y = -2
Users (m)	14 ▸ 21 y/y = +7	26 ▸ 31 y/y = +5	6 ▸ 4 y/y = -2

No other significant changes for other brands were recorded over this time, suggesting that the only ones showing any change were those with high or low BVS. The changes in these brands were directionally in line with brand momentum theory, with solid evidence from Indeed and Jobcentre Plus. The unexpected changes in prompted awareness started us thinking that BVS can drive (or predict) future brand awareness. The BVS also remained steady for the full 12 months for all the brands, suggesting that high and low velocity can last a year or more and that it's not just a short-term blip which may be associated with advertising campaigns.

Case Study 2 – Online Moneysaving Apps

While tracking a wide range of brands offering money-saving apps and on the lookout for brands with high or low BVS, we did notice that MyVoucherCodes, an online voucher code company founded in 2006, was showing a low score (BVS=53). Our research also indicated that consumers were moving away from discount codes, as they were seen by users as unreliable and often replicated offers already available online. So, as we anticipated, a year later the brand experienced a reduction in the number of users (-2% y/y/), along with a slight decline in awareness.

On a more positive note, Honey, the deal-finding extension for Chrome, was acquired by PayPal in 2019 and recorded the highest velocity (BVS = 75) around that time. A year later, as expected, it had made gains in terms of brand awareness, interest and usage (+2% y/y), and was the only brand to achieve all three of these over the test period.

Year-on-Year Changes in Awareness, Interest and Mass

	High Momentum Honey BVS = 75	Low Momentum Voucher Codes BVS = 53
Prompted Awareness	26 ▸ 31 y/y = +5	47 ▸ 44 y/y =-3
Interest	20 ▸ 23 y/y = +3	32 ▸ 30 y/y =-2
Users (m)	16 ▸ 18 y/y = +2	26 ▸ 24 y/y =-2

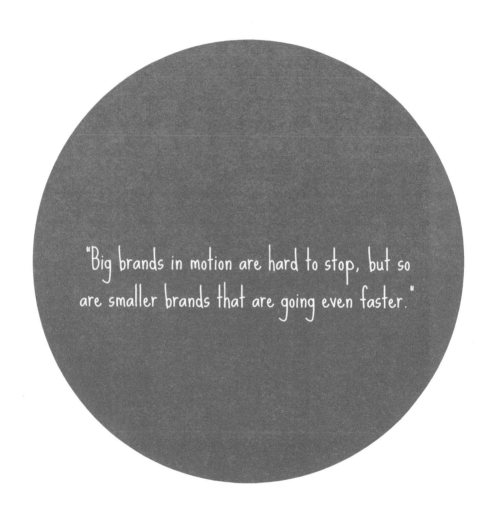

"Big brands in motion are hard to stop, but so are smaller brands that are going even faster."

Chapter VI
Creating Velocity

Since power equals force times speed, if the athlete learns to make faster movements he increases his power, even though the contractile pulling strength of his muscles remains unchanged. Thus, a smaller man who can swing faster may hit as hard or as far as the heavier man who swings slowly.

Bruce Lee

In this chapter, I'll delve into the factors that shape BVS and their transformative benefits. Momentum isn't just about sales or customer growth; it goes beyond that and shapes the internal health and culture of your entire business operation. I'll demonstrate why it's the most critical metric for understanding consumers and achieving your business objectives.

Dual Perspectives

*If you don't give the market the story to talk about,
they'll define your brand's story for you.*

David Brier

**People want to feel empathy and have confidence in
their brand choices and will look for clues to confirm or
refute their judgements. The signals that brands send
to existing and potential buyers are vitally important in
driving brand growth – I would argue more important
than the overt claims and messages they often make.**

Our research points to a number of factors driving brand velocity and our perceptions of growing and declining brands. It seems that there are certain qualities that help to project growing brands, and this chapter is concerned with understanding the factors that drive and create BVS.

In studying BVS and how brands grow, there are two distinct elements in the consumer's mind that can be viewed as two perspectives required to generate and create brand velocity.

1. **The WorldView: The Social Context**
   This is how people see the brand in a broader social context, such as who buys or uses it, whether it is popular, whether it is fashionable or desirable, when to use it and how. In essence, it is what people learn from others or believe is happening in the outside world. Moreover, brands that display altruism and support for society

have seen remarkable growth in recent years, which is also strongly linked with a high brand velocity.

2. **MyView: Experiences and Emotions**

   Brands send signals to us in many ways, which alter our perceptions, our relationships, and our interest in a brand. *Brand Vitality* (excitement, innovation, etc.) is one of the most important factors in driving velocity. However, our personal experiences, beliefs, and perceptions of the category and the brands within it, also have a role to play in altering and improving brand velocity.

Clearly, some brand perceptions, experiences and emotions are important to marketers and the success of brands. However, I believe that marketers tend to pay insufficient attention to the 'WorldView' which rightly or wrongly drives many of the choices we make as individuals (albeit often subconsciously).

The Anatomy of Brand Velocity (BVS)

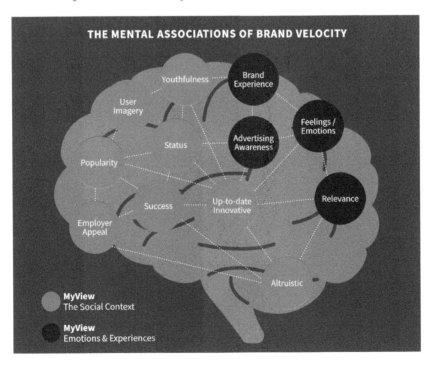

As illustrated above, velocity consists of the WorldView (e.g., social fitness, user imagery and altruism) and MyView, which is more focused on our own experiences and viewpoints, including feelings, brand relationship and experiences.

All these elements have been selected because they have the strongest impact on brand velocity and creating momentum. However, both our minds and the world are dynamic, so it is important to note that these components will change slowly over time and will also change in importance from market to market (e.g., Food and Drink, Technology, Luxury etc.) and so will have slightly different emphasis and meaning in each market.

The creation of velocity is largely a reflection of the company's business activities, the product, and the investment in sales and marketing. Building velocity isn't rocket science; it involves focusing on the building blocks of business growth and making sure the consumer is aware and in tune with these activities and conscious of your brand direction.

The 6 Key Drivers of Velocity

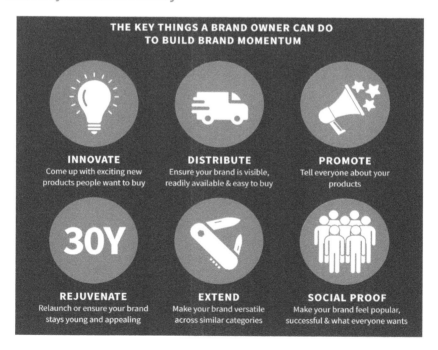

The 6 key drivers of velocity and momentum are well-known to marketers. However, Rejuvenation may surprise some. This is discussed shortly, but in brief, we have discovered that the perceived age of the user (user-image) of a brand is strongly linked to brand velocity. In other words, age drives perceptions of whether a brand is growing or declining. Brands often age with time and successful re-branding invariably rejuvenates the brand by attracting new and younger customers. Whilst CMOs can be heavily involved in all these areas, I believe their three key roles should be to promote, rejuvenate and help create social proof for the brand.

WorldView – The Social Context

*Every generation laughs at the old fashions
but follows religiously the new.*

Henry David Thoreau, Walden

Social perceptions and beliefs comprise four main components: Brand Vitality, User Imagery, Social Proof and Altruism, which cumulatively I refer to as the WorldView of a brand. These societal perceptions combine to create a powerful influence on our perceptions and behaviours, which are explained below.

Brand Vitality

Vitality is essentially the degree to which a brand demonstrates it is alive and kicking. This can relate to brand visibility and how widely available it is, but it also relates to communication and the degree to which the brand engages with customers. Unfortunately, metrics like prompted brand awareness, tell us little about people's thoughts and feelings. However, in our brand trackers, we find that brands that are perceived as having 'advertised recently' are more likely to be growing than those not actively advertising.

Vitality is crucial for maintaining positive brand perceptions:

1. Brands that exude energy and youthfulness typically achieve higher growth. We often find that vitality correlates with the user imagery and is frequently perceived as young-at-heart, enthusiastic and adventurous.

2. Innovation is another key part of vitality. Whilst it may offer new revenue streams for brands, from a customer point of view, it demonstrates that a brand is moving with the times and shows that it is healthy. Brands that innovate tend to be seen as more exciting. Vitality is also linked with image attributes like fun, innovative and creative.

The act of doing (advertising, innovating, communicating, etc.) alone is often good enough to create vitality. In other words, while creativity can play a key role in your advertising effectiveness, this is reason to believe that the exact nature of your advertising messages isn't necessarily important. For example, many of the most effective campaigns do not mention the quality or uniqueness of the product. Conversely, a lack of marketing activity over time will likely lead to the brand being forgotten and becoming a distant memory.

However, a brand's ability to drive growth or maintain its BVS will partly depend on how the consumer perceives the category as a whole. A growing category will likely lead to all brands achieving higher BVS scores, while a declining or low-interest market will lead to depressed brand velocity scores for many brands within the sector. This is why you can't always take the BVS in isolation as a measure of growth. It also highlights the important role of the market leader, who will often shape the perceptions of the category, and the leader's responsibility to help drive market perceptions.

User Imagery – Stereotyping

Often overlooked by today's researchers and marketers, user imagery refers to the type of people who are seen to use a product or service, such as athletes, celebrities, or parents. We all find it easy and natural to create stereotypes in our minds. We're not talking here about personalities but the well-established stereotyping in society, such as by age, gender and ethnicity. For example, signalling a young age can be important in fashion retailing, especially for the younger generations. This signalling process is important, as it not only tells someone if the product is relevant, it also offers some of the strongest clues as to whether a brand is growing or declining in the consumer's mind.

User imagery is the consumer's definition of a brand's target market. It's a great way to see if your marketing is working and targeting the right people and if there are any gaps or weaknesses. How we individually and collectively see the brand users drives our brand perceptions in the following ways:

1. **Empathy** with the perceived users of a brand can create interest and affinity. In surveys, 'a brand for me' is often highly correlated with usage and purchasing behaviour in virtually every study we have conducted.
2. A youthful user image can signal **Brand Vitality**. This appears to be the most important factor in driving momentum. A brand with an older user image is a strong indicator of a failing brand in the consumer's mind (although there are exceptions).
3. The broader the user image (i.e. for multiple user types), the more popularity it can convey, adding further support to Social fitness.
4. User imagery can also convey brand fitness characteristics such as 'Success' or signal 'Wealth'. These can be more important for premium and luxury brands and markets.

Creating the right user imagery is critical for growing velocity and long-term success, and yet very few businesses do this! In his book *The Psychology of Persuasion* Robert Cialdini highlights the fact that social proof is more powerful when we are observing the behaviour of people just like us – he calls it '*Peer-suasion*'. This *peer-suasion* goes a long way to explain the growth of user-created content and the use of 'ordinary' people we see in advertising in recent years.

User Imagery – Age Perception

One of the most fascinating findings in our research on user imagery is the importance of the perceived age of the average user of a brand. We discovered that growing brands were seen as having a user age profile on average a staggering 19 years younger than those of declining brands. This dramatic difference in age was so profound that user imagery has become a fundamental part of brand momentum theory and practice.

Forever Young

In a recent client survey amongst a sample of UK adults aged 18-65+, the average age of all the respondents was 45. We asked them about the age they felt they were and the age they would like to be. The results back up other research and showed that respondents felt physically four years younger than their actual age (i.e. 41 years old). Mentally/emotionally they actually felt even younger – on average nine years younger (i.e. 36 years rather than 45 years old). These findings support the idea that we feel younger than we are. Furthermore, when asked what age they would ideally like to be, this reality-gap becomes even more extreme, with the most common age given being 30 years, with a mean age of 31 (i.e. 14 years younger).

This age self-analysis distortion carries on throughout life – why not try it on yourself right now? Physically and mentally, do you feel younger than you are? Fascinatingly, this same age distortion is overlaid onto our perceptions of the profile of users of growing and declining brands. This has important implications for marketers. The same sample of adults expressed the view that users of declining brands were on average 49 years of age, some 4 years older than the average age of the sample. This finding is in line with other studies we have conducted and leads to the notion that an older user image is often synonymous with decline. On the other hand, the user profile of growing brands was seen as having an average age of 30 – even younger than the sample's ideal age of 31.

In this study, differences by age group need to be factored in, such as the fact that some young people want to be older than they are. However, overall, it clearly shows that there is a significant perceived age difference between growing and declining brands in terms of user imagery. Therefore, this should form part of any brand evaluation and strategy.

Social Proof

These signals refer to the cues consumers pick up about a brand's social status. Sources include marketing, PR, word of mouth (WOM), recommendations, online reviews, availability, and popularity indicators. Signalling social proof works on several different levels;

- **Popularity and familiarity:** We are social creatures and we are programmed to learn from others, often making decisions based on our beliefs. Research shows that many brand buyers appear to choose the market leader simply because it is the most popular or established.

    Word of mouth and online reviews play an increasing role in helping us form our opinions and make our choices. Not only do they help suggest or promise something about the quality or fitness of the brand, but they also support its sense of popularity. However, what we see other people doing is just as important as what they say, and this is why brands spend so much time and money helping to make their brands stand out! Apple designed their laptops to show the logo up the right way up for anyone seeing the person use the laptop (whilst being upside down for the user). This is because social proof is more important, i.e. in the case of Apple, making sure others know you're using an Apple laptop.

    I think the idea of social proof is captured well by Daniel Kahneman in his book, *Thinking Fast and Slow*:

    A reliable way to make people believe in falsehoods is frequent repetition because familiarity is not easily distinguished from truth.

- **Success and status:** We all seem to like winners, and being associated with success is human nature. Although we occasionally like to root for the underdog, that doesn't mean we want to be them. Growing brands are strongly associated with success and winning, but declining brands are doomed as they are typically seen as failures by the customer. Success in itself can also convey brand attributes such as quality, effectiveness and desirability.

These social signals also appear to enhance value perceptions. Our research shows that growing brands are often considered "worth paying more for" and "worth investing in". These elements increase demand, potentially influencing consumers to pay premiums, buy company shares, or even generate interest in working for the company.

Altruism Does You a World of Good

A brand displaying altruism has grown in importance as an influencing factor in recent years. While brands have varying imagery and values, there is growing evidence that brands with some element of focus on altruism (benefiting others and society at large) attain stronger positive perceptions and growth. Clearly, the drivers vary somewhat by market/category and will evolve over time, but in general, our latest research on altruism show that it is influential and worth incorporating. Remember, the perception of altruism can be wide reaching. Any reaction making people feel happy or of solving a problem can help to create a sense of altruism and goodwill in its brand values.

Of course, charities' central proposition is altruism. And many commercial brands have woven an element of support for good causes into their image for decades. But growing levels of inequality across the world have fed into a feeling that promoting fairness and kindness is more important than ever. Many brands have moved into this space by committing to Corporate Social Responsibility (CSR), operating ethically, supporting communities and fostering diversity. Protecting the environment and lowering the carbon footprint of a brand's activity have, for a growing number of consumers, become a key factor in brand choice.

Our research has found a strong link between being perceived as doing good and brand velocity. This seems to be corroborated by World Advertising Research Centre (WARC) in a paper titled *What we know about the theories of brand growth*. This paper references a 2020 Kantar Consulting study that found that altruism-focused brands outperformed the average by nearly twofold, with a 175% valuation increase over 12 years. These whopping numbers clearly show the benefit of an altruistic approach and that doing good things can offer a win-win situation for everyone.

Already though, there are clear signs that lazy or misleading attempts to attach altruism to a brand are a grave mistake, and can lead to a brand being seen as less ethical than if they had never tried to attach that halo to the brand. Claims of greenwashing (misleading or false environmental credential claims) or sportswashing (nations attempting to drown out human rights abuses through sports sponsorship) are regularly reported, and have created sharper antennae amongst consumers as to the veracity of altruistic claims, and the motives behind making them. CSR has all too often become a tick-box exercise in the shareholders' report. So, what may seem like a good win strategy for a brand should only be entered into with genuine commitment, or you will get found out.

MyView – Experiences and Emotions

I want to keep my attractiveness as long as I can. It has to do with vitality and energy and interest.

Jacqueline Bisset

MyView is the term we have coined for the personal perceptions and beliefs that relate to an individual's experiences of a brand. As a result, it is less focused on the brand's role in a social context. The three key components of MyView are Brand Fitness, Brand Experiences, and Brand Emotions.

Brand Fitness

Brand fitness reflects the credentials and health of a brand, typically within a category. For example, you may love eating at KFC, but you probably wouldn't want to buy a car from them if they ever went into production (well, only with a great deal of convincing!). Not only would you be wary, but I suspect you probably wouldn't be willing to pay a fortune for it either. Brand credibility or fitness plays a part in momentum but also explains why some brands find it difficult to operate successfully in multiple markets. Three aspects of a brand are important here:

- **Brand salience:** We tend to simplify most things in life by assigning them a label or group. In the case of brands, we tend to assign them to a market, category or sub-category. Daniel Kahneman popularised System 1 (autopilot) and System 2 (slow thinking – using reasoning and logic to solve problems) in his book *Thinking, Fast and Slow*. We shop on autopilot most of the time, so how quickly brands come to mind in a situation is important. The key to growth for most brands is to become autopilot brands. This salience can elevate our perceptions of brand status but also makes it more likely that individuals will pay full price for such brands and brands of choice.

- **Brand status:** Most brands are in competitive markets, and consumers often have a tendency to place brands in a pecking order in terms of status and desirability. This can be related to the strength and position of a brand within a category (e.g., market leader), but it can also be more about its size and stature, brand story, and success. While any social perceptions and our WorldView will impact brand fitness, this measure is more about personal beliefs and responses to the brand. This status can also relate to perceived success in the category and the desire to have a job working for that brand or pay more for that brand than others.

- **Brand distinctiveness:** Humans are social creatures influenced by what we perceive others think and do. In the realm of brands, this means that standing out matters. The concept of Distinctive Brand Assets (popularised by Jenni Romaniuk) has become essential for brand-builders. These assets – think packaging, messaging, colours, and characters – enhance distinctiveness and differentiation. When you think of a brand, what immediately comes to mind is likely a key distinctive brand asset. The stronger this asset, the more memorable your brand becomes.

Monzo's bright pink (coral) card is a prime example; its unique colour makes it noticeable, suggesting greater popularity. While less crucial for direct growth than other elements, distinctiveness amplifies advertising effectiveness and catches our attention which can help boost a brand's trajectory.

Brand Experiences

Positive and negative experiences and emotions can make or break a brand. Declining brands are often associated with failure, and a poor experience or complaint is a surefire way to lose customers.

As consumers, we all start out knowing very little about the brands we buy and use, but over time, this changes. Interestingly, most non-users of a brand cite not knowing enough about the brand as the main reason for not using it. Overall, consumers don't often reject brands outright but simply require help getting them over the line. The moment of truth for most brands comes when consumers first experience a brand, and this is when opinions tend to formulate and harden, either for the better or worse. The more primed we are when we try something, the greater our expectations are, and the more likely we will have a positive experience.

Product quality and service are vital components for most brands. Customers are far more likely to recommend a brand (i.e. become promoters) if they have a positive experience and a strong emotional connection. Our research shows that poor experiences and the number of complaints kill momentum and create more decliners. Most consumers say they would rather do business with a competitor after more than one bad experience.

And of course, good and bad opinions about a brand travel faster and further than ever before. Before the online world, a bad experience in a restaurant would travel as far as your friends and family – now, potentially, the whole world knows about it.

Brand Emotions

We experience many emotions daily, but according to leading researchers, they can be simplified down to seven basic emotions: joy, excitement, surprise, trust, disgust, sadness, and anger. We can use these same emotions to capture people's sentiment towards a brand and what it offers. At the most basic level, people's reactions can be either positive or negative and are at the heart of all our decision-making.

Emotions, both positive and negative, are what make us care. They not only affect our choices but also strongly influence our attention and motivate our behaviours. Similarly, emotions and feelings have a strong impact on our interactions and relationships with brands. They explain why we take notice of certain types of advertising more than others or why we feel more loyal to certain brands. This is why so many successful TV adverts focus on emotional rather than rational messages.

Overall, as we shall see later, emotion encapsulates the energy we feel towards a brand and is a key driver of brand momentum and BVS.

Positive Brand Image

Perhaps the most interesting aspect of brand velocity is whether it creates a positive brand image or if the positive brand image creates velocity. If you believe a brand is growing, it will probably possess many positive qualities. In contrast, a brand in decline is likely to be creating more negative perceptions. Creating velocity appears to drive many positive aspects, the most important of which is 'success' in all its connotations.

Image Attributes of Growing Brands.

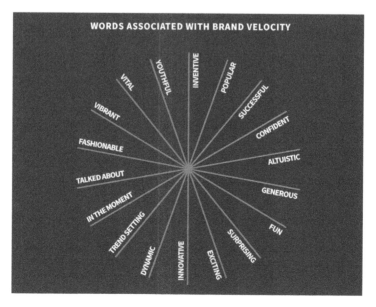

Impact, Benefits and the BrandBank

Momentum is ultimately about attracting more users to a brand, extending its life, and improving brand perceptions. But momentum does a lot more than this. It can also enhance loyalty and advocacy and uniquely foretell future growth and performance.

Our research into the drivers of BVS and momentum has found some other unexpected benefits. Here we look at what they are and why or how they have come about.

So let's first look at how brand momentum creates a sustained effect over time. Mass and velocity are inextricably linked and both fuel each other. I call this the Momentum Continuum or Loop and this is in effect the engine that drives growth and gives it additional power and longevity.

As illustrated overleaf, business activities add energy into the system. For example, an advertising campaign will energise consumers and enhance perceptions (e.g., raise BVS) in the short-term, which will lead to increased numbers of customers. But it doesn't stop there. This increase in customer numbers creates additional social proof and, ultimately more velocity by injecting new life into the momentum continuum. This process continues but the effects will diminish as each activity fades in consumers' memories.

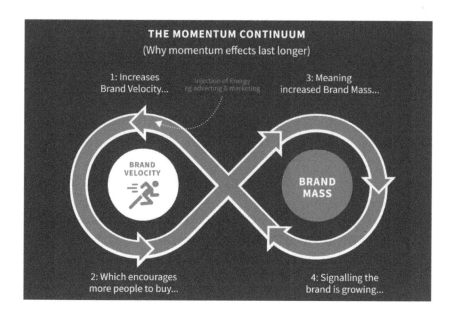

THE MOMENTUM CONTINUUM
(Why momentum effects last longer)

1: Increases
Brand Velocity...

Injection of Energy
eg advertising & marketing

3: Meaning
increased Brand Mass...

BRAND
VELOCITY

BRAND
MASS

2: Which encourages
more people to buy...

4: Signalling the
brand is growing...

Boosting Loyalty

One of the key findings of our research into momentum was the discovery that loyalty is also a factor and a key benefit of momentum. Indeed, the results showed that people who thought a brand was growing were over three times more likely to claim to be loyal to that brand.

In hindsight, this probably makes sense when you ask yourself, "Why should consumers be loyal to a declining brand?". During some focus groups exploring how people feel about growing and declining brands, we found that declining brands were often associated with failure. They were often considered brands that had "failed to keep up with the times" or "were no longer relevant" and had probably not innovated or kept their communications up to date.

Buying a brand is often an investment of some kind for many people, as it often entails paying a bit more for a (sometimes but not always...) superior product over a shop's own brand, or in preference to a cheaper or inferior product. This is particularly true in luxury markets, where connotations of success and craftsmanship are more important. So, when investing in a brand, consumers are looking for one that will be around and give them kudos. When talking to consumers and their definition of declining brands, we found that these brands were often seen as "failures" or had lost relevance with society or the category.

In addition to finding that people are attracted to growing and avoid declining brands, we also discovered that brands that don't reflect people's values and ideas were even more likely to be avoided. In both the US and the UK, we found that almost half (45%) would avoid brands that don't align with their values and ideas, and this also appears to help explain why loyalty affects perceptions of relevance.

Popularity and Spreading the Word

As we saw at the beginning of this book, the Net Promoter Score is an important metric in many boardrooms and is used in many customer experience programmes to measure the strength of a relationship with a brand and the likelihood of recommending it. Thousands of businesses use it today to measure and track how their customers perceive them, after Bain and Company first developed it in 2003.

NPS is measured with a single-question survey and reported as a score from -100 to +100. A higher score is desirable. It measures customer perception based on one simple question:

"How likely is it that you would recommend [Organisation X/Product Y/Service Z] to a friend or colleague?"

Respondents give a rating between 0 (not at all likely) and 10 (extremely likely) and fall into one of three categories depending on their responses, as follows:

1. **Promoters** are those who give a rating of 9 or 10 and are typically the most loyal and enthusiastic of customers.
2. **Passives** are those who give a rating of 7 or 8. They are satisfied with the product or service received but not happy enough to be considered promoters.
3. **Detractors** are the lowest-rated customers, scoring from 0 to 6. These are disappointed or unhappy customers who are unlikely

to buy that brand again and may even discourage others from buying it.

The Net Promoter Score is calculated by subtracting the number of Detractors from the number of Promoters.

While NPS has been widely adopted across many major brands, especially in the US, it has one fundamental flaw: it can only be applied to people who are customers/users of the brand, which limits its use to brand builders. BVS, on the other hand, can be applied to anyone aware of a brand, and typically, BVS can be calculated separately for users and non-users, for a more detailed understanding of a brand and its customers.

Despite this setback of only being applicable to users, Bain and Co. have argued that NPS is a good growth predictor and have provided numerous examples of its ability to show growth potential. On their website, NetPromoterSystem.com, Bain and Co. also claim that when they have analysed publicly available growth figures, NPS explained roughly 20% to 60% of the variation in organic growth between brands in the same market. On average, the leader with the highest NPS outgrew its competitors by a factor greater than two.

After investigating Vision One's *BrandBank*, we examined the relationship between BVS and NPS. Our analysis of brand velocity does conclude, in spite of our reservations above, that NPS is one of the more robust metrics associated with growth and BVS. For this reason, we believe that BVS and NPS make an ideal combination of metrics when looking to create business growth and momentum.

There are many similarities between the BVS and the NPS approaches. NPS is liked by many for being a metric that provides regular feedback and tracks the company's performance in the customers' minds. Also, it can inspire internal teams to grow the company and become more successful. We believe BVS is an excellent addition to any company using NPS, but we use it more to focus on brand and marketing activities.

The table opposite compares the features and benefits of BVS and NPS.

Features and Benefits of BVS

	BVS	NPS
The Question	"Growing, declining or static?" (3 pt)	"Likelihood to recommend?" (11 pt)
Focus on growth	Focusing on activities that enhance the perceptions of growth	Treating customers as you want to be treated
Scope	Non-customer and customers	Customers only
Who For (Function)	• CEOs & C-suite • Brand and Marketing • Finance/Investors	• CEOs & C-suite • Customer Services • Innovation/product team
Acquisition	All methods (unrestricted) i.e. growth by any means	Growth through loyalty and word of mouth
People Focus	Users and non-users Growers and Decliners	Promoters and Detractors

While NPS is largely focused on customer-facing teams and functions, BVS is focused on the marketing and growth functions of the business. I believe momentum provides an excellent indicator of brand equity and the health of a business, and at some point in the future, I believe it could be adapted to become a means of valuing brands on the balance sheet.

Velocity Improves Talent

How well a company is perceived isn't just restricted to the public but can also improve recruitment and employee engagement.

Research shows that brands with a high BVS have many more people interested in working for them and, as such, are likely to attract more talented individuals. When interviewed, 14% of the public were interested in working for a brand that was seen as growing, and this is more than double the 6% who were interested despite not seeing the brand as growing. This increase in interest not only means that recruitment would be easier but that employers are more likely to attract a higher quality talent pool of candidates across their business.

Case Study – Rio Tinto

I stumbled upon an intriguing story in Nick Liddell's article, 'Brand Purpose – Moving Beyond the Bullshit' (Sep 2015).[10] In it, he shares a fascinating tale about Rio Tinto, the major mining and materials industry player. Rio Tinto is a global giant with a colossal workforce of over 90,000 employees spanning 35 countries. What caught my eye is how they leveraged momentum to revamp their recruitment and retention strategies – a noteworthy approach in such a vast and diverse corporate landscape.

In 2011, faced with a complex history and heightened market pressures, the company decided to redefine its core purpose, aiming to attract and retain the upcoming generation of miners.

The former company motto, 'Do the right thing', was replaced by the more dynamic 'Moving Mining Forward'. This fresh purpose embodied a sense of momentum and aimed to provide the company with a positive narrative, highlighting continuous innovation, shared value creation and contributions to the end market.

This revitalised purpose triggered a substantial shift in the company's recruitment and employee engagement approach. Rio Tinto took the bold step of challenging conventional perceptions of life within a mining company, casting their employees as heroes in a recruitment campaign that aimed to showcase a more humane side of the company. The campaign's impact surpassed expectations, exceeding targets by over 150% and earning recognition with the 'Best of Breed Graduate Recruitment' awards in South Africa, Mongolia and Australia.

As the saying goes, the proof is in the pudding. In February 2014, the *Financial Times* featured an article spotlighting the transformation of Rio Tinto under the leadership of CEO Sam Walsh, the visionary behind the brand's renewed purpose:

Whichever way you look at Rio Tinto's results, you sense the hallmarks of a renaissance under Walsh. The true value will be found not by what he has taken out of the business but what he has put in: an attitude and spirit of absolute improvement.

A strong brand BVS can also greatly impact employee morale and engagement, and companies with highly engaged workforces are 21% more profitable and productive. According to Gallup's meta-analysis, businesses that scored the highest on **employee engagement showed 21 per cent higher levels of profitability** than units in the lowest quartile. Companies with highly engaged workforces also scored 17% higher on productivity.

In the same way that BVS attracts talent, Vision One's research into BVS has shown that consumers are more likely to invest in and buy shares in high-velocity brands. This makes a great deal of sense as we surely all look for value growth in our investments and have little interest in investing in brands with a negative trajectory. This also helps explain why consumers claim to be prepared to pay more for brands with a high BVS.

How You Lose Velocity

Fashion is always of the time in which you live. It is not something standing alone. But the grand problem, the most important problem, is to rejuvenate women. To make women look young. Then, their outlook changes. They feel more joyous.

Coco Chanel

Successfully prolonging brand health requires eliminating negative forces that slow down or even reverse momentum. Poor brand experiences and bad publicity have a detrimental effect, but being boring and losing relevance are the biggest silent killers.

Think of that favourite neighbourhood restaurant that has had the same menu for a decade. It's reliable, but the lack of change or surprise makes it lose its initial spark. Brands, like restaurants, need to keep things fresh and their menus evolving to keep their customers returning.

While looking at the data for possible explanations as to why brands decline, the validity of BVS was confirmed by a low score being linked to lapsed users. The higher the number of lapsed users (and fewer current users), the lower the BVS. This made sense intuitively and helped to prove the value of BVS as a measurement. Let me explain.

1. A brand with many lapsed users clearly hasn't been able to retain customers. It's a classic example of a leaky bucket that hasn't

been plugged. As brands get older, the chances of customers lapsing increases, but a strong BVS and keeping the brand/product relevant, will help to retain customers.

2. A low BVS is a warning sign of a weakened offering or a problem in retaining customers. A brand that constantly has to recruit new customers to stay still is not a viable brand in the long run. It also explains why so many marketers focus on retaining customers. Clearly, by not losing customers, a brand will maintain a stronger BVS and retain momentum for longer.

3. It also shows that there is a behavioural aspect to brand momentum. In other words, momentum and BVS aren't just in the mind; they are related to real behavioural changes/differences – a strong BVS means fewer lapsed customers.

Overall, this means that strong brands and achieving momentum require minimising the number of lapsed users. Furthermore, if you want another good indicator of brand health, simply look at the number of lapsed customers your brand has.

Lapsed Buyers Reduce Velocity

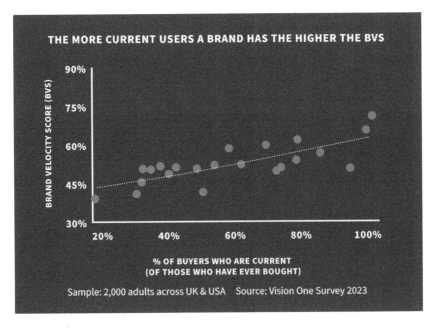

THE MORE CURRENT USERS A BRAND HAS THE HIGHER THE BVS

Sample: 2,000 adults across UK & USA   Source: Vision One Survey 2023

You may recall that I started this book with the fate of Monarch Airlines. If a market is in decline and being surpassed by another, this will be difficult to overcome. Unfortunately, if you are the market leader, it will mean the responsibility to address the market issues will be yours. However, brands cannot grow without BVS, nor will they find it easy to change their image for the better until they possess at least some momentum to make the turnaround credible. Just ask yourself why a failing brand should be credible or trustworthy. People avoid risks, especially when it comes to spending money, and the lower your momentum, the higher the risk your brand will be.

Losing or destroying momentum is similar to the way some personal relationships start to feel dull or even fall apart. I suspect the most common causes of relationship breakdowns are that one or both parties have stopped making an effort or that someone else has come along to steal someone's interest. I think our relationship with brands is very similar. Keeping any relationship interesting means showing each other interest, attention and affection. Not spending time together, ignoring feelings, and even neglecting each other's needs are bound to contribute to feelings of boredom. In the same way, brands need to forge relationships with people; without them, momentum is lost.

Our research showed that one of the biggest differences between growing and declining brands was that declining brands were significantly lower in delivering the need we refer to as 'Informs'. This suggests that a lack of communication is a key reason for their demise.

In 2024, a collaboration led by creative measurement firm System1, strategic consultancy eatbigfish, and marketing effectiveness expert Peter Field, with their latest findings unveiled at WARC's Creative Impact conference in New York, concluded that dull US adverts were effectively wasting $228 billion. The root cause of this failure is what many insight experts have known for a long time: a failure to trigger the desired emotion in the viewer of an advert will kill its effectiveness, and the same is true for brands.

The three main reasons for a loss of momentum are:

1. **Loss of interest**
   This is a constant battle for brand owners – any fall-off in advertising and communication plays to the natural forgetfulness and fickle nature of consumers, and so can irrevocably damage brands and cause a fatal loss of momentum. Brands must be visible and readily available, or they will be forgotten.

2. **Irrelevant or uninteresting**
   Brands seen as "Boring" and "Dated" lack interest and relevance to many. These are significant indicators that brands are losing customers and heading for the rocks, and they play a big part in the demise of many brands.

3. **Bad news or experiences**
   Declining brands are much more likely to have high levels of complaints and poor experiences. PricewaterhouseCoopers' *Future of Customer Experience* survey 2017/18[11] claims that 32% of all customers in the US would stop doing business with a brand they loved after just one bad experience. Negative reviews online are having an increasingly detrimental impact on a brand's standing.

   Conversely, the positive PR obtained by good customer service (e.g., speed, convenience, knowledgeable help and friendly service) is transmitted exponentially wider via positive online reviews..

   As Bill Gates once said, *"If I was down to the last dollar of my marketing budget, I'd spend it on PR!"*

There are many stories of brands losing momentum, and bad news travels fast. Two examples of bad news destroying a brand's reputation and killing momentum almost overnight are:

Perrier sparkling water: One of the most extreme cases – in 1990, when Perrier was market leader and the iconic, dominant brand, a toxic substance called benzene was discovered in its bottles. The company had little choice but to recall the product. Within a week, Perrier withdrew 160 million bottles worldwide, but fatal damage had been done to the brand's claim of natural purity. The brand still exists today but has never recovered its iconic status or market position.

Volkswagen: In 2015, Volkswagen suffered an international crisis for violating the Clean Air Act by using software that allowed its cars to falsely pass emissions tests. The company had not only violated the law but also damaged customer trust. Even worse, in the early days of the scandal, executives claimed they didn't know about the cheating but later admitted they did. Consumer damages claims, based on this falsehood, are still rumbling on to this day, and the halo of an impeccably efficient and high quality car manufacturer has slipped permanently.

These are extremes, and there are many similar cases. They illustrate that hard-won brand reputations can be destroyed in an instant. As brands age, the number of people who have had a negative experience will grow; brands that don't address this and allow their BVS to decline will shorten their lifespans.

The Trust Delusion

For quite a few years now, I've been asking clients what they believe is the most important aspect of a brand, and I invariably get back the same answer every time: "Trust", they exclaim triumphantly!

This popular answer has always bothered me; it sounds plausible but somehow feels completely wrong because it never really explained any, or many, of the brand choices I have made, nor does it support what customers tell us. For example, I love excitement and thrills – even at my age, put me on a rollercoaster, and I'm in my element. Sure, I want to feel safe, and clearly, anything unsafe may deter us, but this is a reason for not doing something, rather than a reason for choosing safety as the dominant driver. While, as individuals, we are all different, research shows there are some who prioritise safety over happiness or excitement. However, in most cases, these people tend to be the minority within most consumer markets. So why do so many brands put Trust at the top of their list? My guess is that they don't know better or that they are more focused on avoiding failure, rather than success!

The problem isn't so much that brands want to instil confidence; it's more that most marketers put it at the top of their priorities when, in most cases, this isn't what the customer wants. However, I believe this overemphasis or reliance on trust is damaging and makes brands boring! It is precisely the thing that kills brand velocity and a brand that is still evolving.

A question for you... *How many* **boring brands** *can you think of that are* **growing?**

Hopefully, you agree this is a tough question to answer. I believe it could even be argued that being trusted by the customer is a negative thing! Wait, please hear me out before you shout, "No, this can't be true!" But let's see what the research says:

1. One piece of research we recently conducted into the phenomenon of momentum and BVS identified that growing brands were **not** associated with being durable and long-lasting – precisely the qualities you might expect to be positively associated with growth or being a trustworthy brand. The study also found very little evidence of a relationship between trust and momentum. Whilst brand longevity should be the goal for every brand, my beleif is that brands shouldn't play too much on their history or heritage. Brands that focus on their age too much will ultimately stifle their potential for growth (unless it is relevant to their category or brand essence).

2. In 2019, System1's research into brand trust and customer experience (CX) metrics, claimed it found that 'brand trust' was consistently one of the weakest predictors of consumer behaviour for all brands across all industries. In particular, it showed that trust questions were felt to be the hardest for people to answer, and even when they did, respondents themselves had little confidence in their evaluation and admitted they were more likely to be fabricated.

3. Analysis of the Brand Emotion metric from Vision One's *BrandVision* model shows some intriguing results, too. While trust plays a role in generating interest in a brand, it isn't important in terms of driving usage, satisfaction and loyalty. In essence, positive emotions of joy and excitement were far more important than trust. In other words, you need positive emotions to take people down the brand funnel to loyalty. Some initial results suggest that excitement may be the most powerful emotion that drives loyalty.

Joy and Excitement Explain Usage & Loyalty (not Trust)

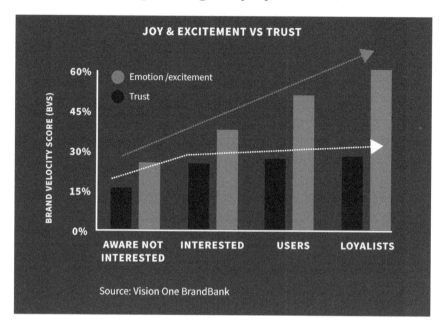

Source: Vision One BrandBank

We can see above that trust rises between non-users who are not interested and those who are interested in a brand – this indicates that trust has some influence in gaining interest. But trust doesn't grow any further beyond this point for users or loyalists. On the other hand, the positive emotions of joy and excitement show a much stronger relationship with every step of the brand funnel. So, it's clear those involved in CX and Customer Relationship Management, or those who want to encourage word of mouth, should focus on emotional connections and address any negative emotions if they are looking for growth.

Taking all this into account and the fact that there is no tangible increase in trust amongst users, I believe there is little evidence that trust is important from a growth perspective for most consumer brands. At best it's a hygiene factor, but it's very likely to be misleading many marketers to be more conservative and functional and forget about more important emotional aspects. Perhaps we should consign trust to Room 101, along with other marketing myths. Its inclusion in brand trackers and customer satisfaction programmes simply suggests it is important, whereas in reality there are far more important metrics for brand owners to concern themselves with. Whenever we do research, emotion is revealed as a strong element in driving consumer choice and commitment. A brand isn't just a logo, product or service – it's a connection, personality, story, and a strong feeling we get for both consumer and B2B brands alike. There is a reassuring calmness to a feeling of trust, so it can rarely be a strong feeling – and this is why it is not a true driver of brand growth and momentum. This is perhaps why we see a much bigger role for trust in B2B markets, and here trust becomes the most important emotion.

We have all witnessed the role momentum plays in our everyday lives. Team and individual sports are the perfect example of where many of us feel and experience it. When a team has momentum, we tend to think or feel a sense of real excitement and a buzz, with the ebb and flow throughout the game. The underdog, with momentum on their side, can seemingly achieve anything. Having momentum is great, and it feels like we are on the crest of a wave.

There is a tendency for people to pay attention to ideas and details that confirm their beliefs. In essence, people favour information that reinforces what they already think or believe, and dismiss that which doesn't. So, in the case of momentum, if we believe a brand is growing, we will find evidence for it – and notice it more in stores or when people are using it. A good example is when looking to buy a new car, we often see many more on the road.

This is why our attitudes and beliefs are hard to change, but it also means that brands with momentum will continue to grow and maintain their momentum into the future. Ultimately, if we believe a brand is successful, popular or growing, we will eventually succumb to these beliefs. We act on these beliefs. So, the perception of momentum can be enough to fuel our behaviours, and ultimately, it will lead to trialling/buying a product or service at some point in the future.

Part 3 Round-up

Mass and velocity need to be at the heart of every brand's strategic aims. Velocity is arguably of more interest to marketers as it is the source of growth – but without mass it is somewhat meaningless.

Velocity provides new thinking into how brands grow. In particular, our research highlights the importance of the WorldView in shaping perceptions and ultimately a brand's potential for growth. It is clear that activity to develop and sustain successful brands needs to focus on creating a strong awareness among the target audience of what other buyers, or potential buyers, are thinking and doing. Focusing on social proof and creating social expectations and beliefs is essential. In the light of this, it is not surprising that the most pervasive new marketing medium is social media and why 'influencers' are now so important for marketers. Don't forget to focus too on popularity, user imagery, social conventions and usage/occasion imagery, as these help to create momentum.

So let's dive into the principles for building brand momentum...

PART 4

BUILDING A MOMENTUM STRATEGY

"Brands are powerful forces in our lives. They go far beyond logos and slogans, they create promises, act as mental shortcuts, and influence how we feel and think."

Introduction
Momentum is Success

Branding demands commitment; commitment to continual reinvention; striking chords with people to stir their emotions; and commitment to imagination. It is easy to be cynical about such things, much harder to be successful.

Sir Richard Branson

You may recall that I started this book with a quote by Professor Snape in *Harry Potter and the Philosopher's Stone*, where he explains to Harry Potter and his class what he will be teaching them in potions classes that year. This analogy might seem far-fetched to some, but it precisely resembles brand momentum and what the BVS can do to help brands and those involved in brand management. For example;

- To *Bewitch the Mind* means making the brand appear more attractive to them
- To *Ensnare the Senses* is to manage expectations and what people experience using a brand
- To *Bottle Fame* is about raising popularity and word of mouth
- *Brewing Glory* is the sense of winning and success
- To *Put a Stopper in Death* is the extension of the life of the brand

Now that you understand momentum and its benefits and know how to measure it, the remainder of this book is dedicated to providing essential hints and tips on building a momentum strategy for yourself.

I recognise that every brand is unique, each with its own strengths, weaknesses and challenges. The following chapters will provide the building blocks and ideas to help you prepare and implement a successful strategy to drive your brand and marketing plans. In essence, with momentum and BVS, you should start to experience the following:

1. The brand will begin to attract more new customers.
2. Marketing will gradually become more effective as your customer base grows.
3. Brand awareness and interest will grow, subsequently improving your brand funnel.
4. Brand image will be boosted across the board, especially in terms of vitality and social fitness.
5. The bottom of the funnel will improve, with increased loyalty and word of mouth.
6. The brand's business will become more appealing as a workplace, attracting talent.
7. The brand should start to become the leader and the one to watch.
8. With increased brand versatility, the brand can better navigate change and become more resilient to competitive threats.
9. The brand's added value will increase consumers' willingness to pay more and attract their investment appeal towards the brand.

In short, you could summarise brand momentum as 'success'. And the amazing thing is that this can all be measured by a single metric (p).

Now that we have an idea of the outcomes we want to achieve, let's examine what a momentum strategy might look like. The next chapter will explore the fundamentals of growing momentum and how they can help you plan your brand reputation and image or even shape the customer experience.

Chapter VII
The Six Principles for Momentum

A momentum strategy means focusing on growth (BVS) and building long-term potential. It doesn't require radically new marketing tools, as it can still use many of today's brand management and marketing principles.

Most companies spend a good deal of their time focused on their tactics and rarely on their strategies. Brand consultant Mark Ritson once said about companies and their lack of a proper strategy, *"What you find in the back of the wardrobe is precisely nothing... for really large brands, there isn't anything there!"* This lack of strategic thinking is commonplace, and it probably explains why there is often an over-emphasis on short-term tactical marketing and why marketers yearn for the next technological breakthrough.

A good strategy is based on a careful diagnosis of a situation; the strategy is the plan to address or fulfil the goals based on that diagnosis. Brand momentum not only provides a means of measurement and for setting goalposts, but it also provides a new framework for building an effective growth strategy. Such a strategy involves improving momentum (i.e. BVS and mass), which will help set companies on an upward trajectory with a long-term plan. When creating or amending your brand's Vision, Mission and Purpose, you must keep these components in mind, ensuring that your brand direction is clear to all.

The following six principles will help you achieve a successful momentum strategy and help maximise your BVS.

1. **Understand Your Customers**
   The customer is the hero. This is about more than just customer service. Consider how brands like Dove or Patagonia put real people and their stories at the heart of their campaigns, turning customers into advocates.

2. **Set Your Sights High**
   Keeping your velocity high means you will be more attractive to switchers. For example, despite its age and size, Google still has strong momentum.

3. **Focus on Acquisition (and others will follow)**
   Innocent Drinks is a brand that started small, selling smoothies at a music festival. Their focus on winning over new customers with their quirky branding and focus on natural ingredients helped them quickly gain popularity. Their early acquisition focus propelled their expansion into major supermarkets. They ended up being acquired by the biggest drinks fish of all, Coca-Cola, but have managed to retain their brand image and values.

4. **Momentum is Self-confident**
   Think of brands like Apple or Nike. They are confident enough that they don't need to boast about their dominance; their presence and the sheer number of their products out in the world speak volumes, but evidence of social proof and the drivers of momentum are essential to grow your velocity and momentum.

5. **Engage Emotions**
   Emotion is essential for developing a relationship with anything or anyone; it makes us care. The emotions of joy and excitement are the powerhouse behind the success of strong brands.

6. Build a Momentum Mindset

This isn't just about lip service. Companies like Amazon are famed for their relentless focus on growth and innovation. This 'momentum mindset' permeates their entire culture, creating the perception of constant upward movement.

Creating momentum starts with the customer, putting them at the heart of the business. The good news is that most marketing directors place customer research as one of their top priorities, with 50% placing it as the first or second most important. This is ahead of efficiency and effectiveness in marketing, which is their No. 2 priority. So putting the customer centre stage shouldn't be hard at all!

However, by customer, I mean all potential customers, and not just the ones you currently have. Far too many businesses focus on their current customers – this is fine if you just want to protect and reduce churn, but it will not help you grow long-term.

If you want the best results and to achieve momentum, it must also radiate from within and across the entire business, from management to frontline staff. If all managers and staff are united in a shared goal, then it stands to reason that it is far more likely to be achievable. By remaining in tune with its customers, their needs and values, a brand will start to gain traction, akin to riding the crest of a wave. If you know what momentum is in your market and how to measure it, you are well on the road to success.

In many cases, building a momentum strategy shouldn't require too much change unless you are not currently advertising or building a brand. For those who are, then it should simply mean placing more emphasis on growing your BVS.

If you want to keep things simple, I suggest you focus on a single goal. In this instance, I recommend focusing on the 2nd principle – Set Your Sights High, which means seeking to have the highest BVS and Momentum in your market or category. If you do, the rest should follow.

The great thing about the momentum approach is that it means the strategy never needs to change – only the tactics! Traditional marketing ideas often imply your brand is rigid (e.g., like a brand diamond) with a definite positioning and values. I've often heard about brands that have some limitations and are untouchable. This overly rigid thinking is both naïve and dangerous for any brand. Change and evolution should be built into every brand's DNA – in fact, if your brand doesn't change and evolve, growth is impossible!

Momentum Principle 1
Understand Your Customers

One of the biggest pleasures I get from working with clients is when research brings new thoughts and ideas to the table. Sure, consumers don't know everything, but by listening carefully, you can often glimpse what consumers want or see in the future. As Neil Armstrong once said, *"Research is creating new knowledge."*

As someone who has spent their whole life researching and exploring the world of consumers, I think it would be amiss not to say a few words on how I believe insights can help brands realise their potential. As you probably know, research can help businesses in many ways, from innovation and discovery to brand tracking. However, to get started, I think understanding what drives momentum in a category, along with measuring and benchmarking your brand's BVS, is most important of all.

Step 1 – Define Your Target Market

You probably already have a clear definition of your target market, but if not, this is the essential first step. A brand strategy should always begin with defining who your ideal customer is. At its very widest, this should include existing market buyers but also potential future buyers – the most successful brands always cast the widest nets.

However, it's vital to paint a clear picture of who they are. Your descriptions should go beyond demographics (e.g., age, gender, etc). They should include identifying and defining their needs and values, making it easier for everyone to identify with them. This information, or persona, will allow you to understand how to position your products or services.

Perhaps the easiest and best way to define your target market is with the 'bullseye' approach, where you have a target with three rings to represent the importance and focus of your attention.

- Bullseye: The core customer (your ideal customer) is at the heart of your business.
- Middle ring: Target customer (top 50% of your buyers)
- Outer ring: All potential long-term customers (category buyers)

These rings represent different segments you should target, especially if you are a young brand. In the early days, you should focus on those most likely to adopt your offering to ensure your marketing is efficient whilst marketing budgets are tight.

However, as we have demonstrated earlier, optimising user image is also a vital part of the jigsaw in achieving momentum, so it is important to ensure your target market and the user image work together.

In most cases, your user image should be younger than your target audience; the exceptions include very young audiences who aspire to become adults. A young image is advantageous because it creates more vitality for the brand. Moreover, when looking into the gap between how older adults feel vs their actual age, our research found that the differences can be dramatic. Our research amongst adults shows that people emotionally feel 9 years younger than they are and aspire to being even younger. Age is often ignored by marketers – so be mindful not to let your image get too old, as this will affect your BVS.

Sensibly, many brands focus on the entry points to the market to help define their core target market. This is often an occasion or situation when people might start using a product or change their product/brand choices. Maximising customer lifetime value often means focusing on the younger ages but not going too niche! Common scenarios might be leaving home to start university or work, getting married and starting a family, or retiring. So, think about the ideal entry age/life stage/situation when, where and why someone would start buying your product – these can be situational or emotional.

Step 2 – Identify the Drivers of Momentum

Understanding what drives BVS, especially for your customers and category buyers overall, is essential. Consumer research is critical if you are looking to understand what motivates and interests them or how to communicate with your audience. Identifying the drivers of momentum and category purchasing can be conducted via focus groups or usage and attitude (U&A) surveys amongst all market buyers.

Every market is different, so understanding what growing and declining mean to consumers within your category is a great way to learn about the signals that are important and associated with being seen as a growing brand. It is also important to help understand how perceptions of growth can be enhanced and communicated in the right way. Paying attention to the seven key components of social and brand perceptions will help ensure you focus on the right things. These are split into WorldView and MyView:

WorldView: Brand Vitality, User Imagery, Social Proof, Altruism.
MyView: Brand Fitness, Brand Experiences, Brand Emotions.

If you work for an international brand, I strongly recommend that you conduct research across different markets, as there are often cultural differences that you need to be mindful of; what works in one country won't always work in another.

Step 3 – Measuring BVS

Once you know the drivers of momentum within your market, your next step should be to understand how well your brand performs against each of these measures. This will tell you where your strengths are currently and where your opportunities might lie for creating additional momentum.

Remember, this will probably change over time, so you will need to repeat the exercise at regular intervals, such as once a year. Generally, you should track your momentum and Brand Velocity Scores at least annually, but if you are looking to evaluate marketing activity, then this might need to be more regularly, such as quarterly or monthly. The advantage of more regular tracking research is that you can also monitor competitor movements more closely, identify early changes and take action when required. However, whilst momentum metrics can move short-term, annual tracking is normally sufficient.

If all you want to measure is your velocity and brand momentum, then simply ask a few questions on a survey amongst a representative sample of the market, to ensure, for example, it reflects the population in terms of age, gender and ethnicity. However, there will be value in collecting more diagnostic information about the customer, the factors that may be driving momentum, and any differences between growers and decliners, if the budget allows.

Step 4 – Setting Your Goals

I often get asked about goal-setting for brands. This can be tricky as it all depends on what the clients are planning and their aims. However, since discovering the drivers of momentum, I have found it so much easier to make recommendations. Brand strategies should be straightforward, and I don't think there could be a simpler strategy than focusing on maximising brand momentum.

Once you have commissioned or undertaken your first survey to measure momentum, you will be able to calculate your own and competitor BVSs. Setting your long-term target could be to achieve the highest momentum in the market. One method I recommend is to look at a brand's closest rival(s) in terms of size and offering and look at the momentum they achieve. You can then set a BVS goal to be higher or at least equal to them. If you are a relatively younger brand, you should always seek to have a higher BVS if you can.

However, if your BVS is below that of many or all of your key competitors, you will need to do something more radical; otherwise, you run the risk of losing market share and falling into decline.

I often hear that brands should change direction in this case, but I would argue strongly against changing any brand's direction, as it rarely works. Reframing the brand can help, but I believe the most successful strategy is to rejuvenate – i.e. make the brand (feel) younger or attract a younger audience. Old Spice is a great example of this:

Old Spice Rejuvenation

Old Spice is a household name in men's shaving and aftershave categories and a brand which that has been around since 1937. In 1990, Old Spice was acquired by Proctor and Gamble for US$300 million, but with an older age profile, the brand and associations with old men was hindering its performance.

In 2009, Old Spice was relaunched with the help of Wieden+Kennedy, Old Spice's creative agency, with a new younger positioning, attitude and voice, with its 'Smell like a man' campaign. This created a remarkable turnaround for the brand, using language that resonated with a younger audience. Despite no changes to the product or the offering, the brand saw its advertising achieve 40 million views on YouTube within a week, and by the year-end, website traffic grew 300% and Google searches increased by 2,000%. The following year, the brand became the #1 body wash brand.

This is a great example of momentum at work. Firstly, brand rejuvenation has helped lower the user age image and create something that speaks to a younger audience. But equally, if not more importantly, it also helped older consumers to see the brand as showing signs of vitality, which is appealing to them. Secondly, I don't believe this is a repositioning in the sense of changing the brand in a new direction – but simply retaining the brand and steering it to a more youthful image.

Impulse – The Measure of Marketing Effectiveness

For those of you looking to assess the impact of advertising and marketing effectiveness, momentum provides a relatively easy means of evaluation. To measure the effectiveness of your momentum strategy and your marketing efforts, you simply need to measure your change in momentum across two periods of time.

The technical name for a change in momentum is called an 'Impulse'. The equation for impulse is $\Delta p = (p2 - p1)$, and simply involves subtracting the current momentum from its previous level. Essentially, the aim of the game is to increase the number of customers you have, whilst preventing your velocity from falling away. The brands that achieve this are the brands that will prosper. We will look at advertising and media in more detail in Chapter VI.

Momentum Principle 2
Set Your Sights High

Brand Visions and Missions rarely come with clear and measurable objectives, nor do they tend to say anything about how the brand will get there. Using momentum and its theories does – it is both the goal and the means.

Momentum is about growing and striving to maximise your brand's potential, ensuring your brand is perceived as healthy and always heading in the right direction. Whatever the age or stage in the brand lifecycle, momentum increases are always possible. Achieving a higher BVS will be much easier if the brand incorporates momentum theory into its brand DNA, along with focusing on the essential signals of vitality, social proof and brand fitness.

Momentum and BVS are both competitive metrics, with winners and losers in the eye of the customer. The more extreme your brand's position in the market (highest and lowest BVS), the more likely your brand performance will be determined by it. Brands in the middle of the market show more random movements but typically show little change in position over time.

Ultimately, brand owners will need to achieve the highest velocity levels if they want to win market share and growth, or at least higher than their key competitors. So, monitoring your BVS and that of your competitors is essential. It's not always possible to have the highest momentum, but as long as you nurture and protect your momentum, your brand should grow.

An important and unexpected finding in our research shows that it's not just fast-growing brands that achieve a high BVS but also some older, established iconic brands that have been around for years – even if they are operating in a stable category!

Goal Setting

Monitoring your BVS at regular intervals via a brand tracking study will be necessary to assess how your brand is faring, set your goals and targets, and help you understand whether you are on the right track.

Goal setting is a critical part of the marketing process. I have often been asked by brand owners how to set targets for their brands, what metrics they should focus on and what to expect. In the past, I've always found this to be tricky. There's rarely a clear answer as it all depends on what the client is planning, what they want to achieve, how much they plan to spend and how they plan to get there. However, since developing our understanding of momentum and its simple framework, I have found it so much easier to make recommendations. The primary goal is simply to constantly maintain and grow your BVS and ensure your momentum continues to grow, but you do need BOTH of these to happen. Brand strategies should be straightforward, and I don't think there could be a simpler strategy than maximising brand velocity. Could target setting get any easier?

Once you have commissioned or undertaken your first momentum survey, you can calculate your BVS and those of your competitors. There are several ways you could set your targets, which include:

1. Setting your long-term target. This could be to achieve the highest BVS and momentum in the market, but if you're not the market leader, this could take years or decades, depending on your market, etc.

2. Possibly more realistically, you could focus on smaller steps to improve momentum and BVS. Perhaps look at your closest rival(s) in terms of size and offering and look at their momentum. Then set yourself a goal where the initial aim is for your BVS to match or be higher than theirs.

   Everything becomes a lot simpler for marketers with a momentum approach, especially when looking for opportunities with brands and customers to target. In most competitive markets, there are vulnerable brands with a weak BVS. Some may be old and tired;

others may be unable to support their brand financially, and some may have complacent management teams or have taken their eye off the ball. Whatever the reason, these brands will be the easiest to steal share from, and their customers will have fewer reasons to stick with them or choose when comparing them with a higher-velocity brand.

3. If you are a relatively young brand and new to the market, you are likely to already have a higher BVS, so you may need to focus more on creating awareness and ensuring your high BVS is converting into mass.

On the odd occasion, I have seen brands create a high BVS but not achieve the levels of mass growth that would be expected. Here, I think it is important to look at your offering and momentum machine to make sure it is working properly and efficiently and that there are no barriers to growth (e.g., poor distribution and lack of availability, insufficient options, inadequate activation or maybe your prices are too high, etc.).

Tips for Start-ups

The introduction phase is important in the brand lifecycle if you want to achieve a high BVS and growth. Ultimately, your highest BVS will be achieved when you first launch your brand, and over time, the natural process means that it will gradually fall from this point. So, it is essential for new brands to maximise the opportunity to build energy from the get-go, as building your BVS later may not be quite so easy.

Over the years, I have found that some brands mistakenly try to skip this phase, attempting to convey trustworthiness and familiarity instead of newness and energy. This misguided thinking rarely works; bypassing the chance to demonstrate your energy effectively robs your brand of one of its greatest early assets. Furthermore, by starting something new, it will be a lot easier to demonstrate within a year or so that your brand is growing because people will be aware of your story and humble beginnings. Prior to launch, prepare a strong launch proposition and follow-up to demonstrate and provide evidence of your growth.

Perceptions of brand vitality are attractive and will encourage people to buy (immediately or sometime in the future). So go out, make a splash, and be proud to be new and exciting! And at some point in the future, you might need to re-inject some vitality to keep the brand moving.

Dealing with a Weak BVS

Brands are always in danger of becoming tired and stale. In this situation, your BVS will become lower than many of your key competitors. You will need to take radical action to get back on the growth path; otherwise, you risk losing share and falling further into decline. As we have stated earlier, decline can all too easily become a death spiral unless quick remedial action is taken.

People often say that brands should change direction when things are not working for them. I don't like this term as it often means steering a different course and moving away from the brand's heritage. Research and experience show that changing people's memories and beliefs is close to impossible – you need to create new beliefs and memories to change perceptions.

Be careful when changing or updating your distinctive brand assets (DBAs). These are your brand's physical and visual elements, such as the logo, brand name and the things consumers have come to rely on to recognise your brand. Most businesses have failings in this area. To jog your memory, here are some well-known stories about failed DBA relaunches.

- A modern-day classic tale is when Tropicana relaunched in 2009 with new packaging which was unrecognised and had to hastily revert to its old design following a 20% loss in sales.
- In 2010, Gap removed the blue box from its logo, which induced outrage from loyal customers, and within six days, the brand moved back to the old logo.
- Name changes can also fail and can take years to recover from. In 2001, Royal Mail developed a new brand, Consignia, to compete with mail delivery companies such as FedEx and UPS. Again, the new name didn't last long.

These examples go to show that changing familiar components needs to be approached with caution. Distinctive assets really shouldn't be touched unless they are broken, and if you change them, these changes should really go under the radar and evolve slowly. You may or may not be aware of this, but Starbucks has changed its logo several times over the years.

Don't Reposition, Rejuvenate!

So, what does work? Keeping the brand youthful is a fundamental part of its momentum strategy, typically conveyed by user imagery and vitality. Many brands achieve this each year by keeping their advertising and marketing relevant and up-to-date.

However, brands often waste time and money trying to change their image. In many cases, I believe this can be futile; we rarely see brands successfully making fundamental changes to their image on our tracking research; it's a very slow process. But be warned, even if you can successfully change perceptions of your brand, you might find it has little or no benefit.

To explain, in physics, there is a well-known law that states that for every action, there is an equal and opposite reaction. This also applies to marketing and brands, and strengthening in one area can lead to weakening in another.

For example, suppose your brand is being criticised for being of poor quality, and you are keen on increasing your brand's quality perceptions. Because quality and value are typically polar opposites, even if you manage to increase your quality perceptions, the chances are that your value-for-money perceptions will fall to compensate.

This equal and opposite reaction is very common. So, how do you get around the problem? It seems that some things are easier to change and are much less likely to create a backlash. The most important of these is momentum. We have yet to see examples of negative reactions to brands improving their momentum. I'm not saying this isn't feasible – I'm sure it is – but at present, I haven't seen any evidence of it.

However, one further thought: given that we know people are more receptive to brands with momentum, it makes far better sense to increase momentum first, as this will enable you to change brand image whilst it is riding the wave. No one listens to people who have lost their credibility – and it's the same for brands.

Momentum Principle 3
Focus on Acquisition

Brand marketing drives sales. ROI and even performance campaigns just don't cut it – as brand marketing outperforms activation campaigns by 80%, according to ROI Genome Analytics Partners.

Not only has the work of Andrew Ehrenberg and Byron Sharp established that brands grow through acquisition, but the same applies to marketing. ROI Genome has concluded that the most successful marketing campaigns focus on brand-building in the upper funnel (i.e. awareness, interest, and purchase) and have a significantly higher long-term impact.

These findings leave little doubt that focusing your business and marketing strategy on growth and acquiring more customers is essential. It also makes logical sense. Not only does brand-building make brands more attractive, but the more people who buy your brand, the more people there are to recommend it. This is why it's so important to focus on growing the number of buyers your brand attracts.

At first sight, acquiring new customers can appear expensive. I believe the one reason many brands focus their marketing on the lower funnel (e.g., current and lapsed customers) is simply that it tends to be cheaper and easier to achieve results. Whilst this is understandable, it is quite short-term and focused on the low-hanging fruit, which serves to simply recycle customers rather than capture new ones. In essence, investing in marketing to current customers only really helps plug the leaky bucket and does not address the main task in hand of filling the bucket.

Marketing and business activities which are known to be effective at attracting more customers to the brand are:

- New distribution channels and expanding into new markets are obvious avenues for growth.
- Finding new usage occasions can often help increase loyalty and attract new customers to the brand.
- Brand extensions can also work, but be mindful of any cannibalisation which may occur.
- Advertising and PR are some of the best ways of reaching prospects by improving BVS and winning new customers.
- Innovation in all its forms. The benefits of new or improved product and service initiatives are well-known and are often at the heart of attracting new users to the brand. They also play a vital role in refreshing brand perceptions and boosting BVS. But be mindful of the fact that most new product launches fail.
- New trends are emerging all the time and offer a simple way to keep the brand topical and moving forward.

Segmenting for Acquisition

The velocity question has an inbuilt means of segmentation, allowing brands to build their strategies and understand different customer groups. Those who think your brand is static or declining are likely to be non-users and the next crop of new customers. So, understanding their barriers should provide important clues on how to inject momentum and encourage them to buy.

The question provides the crucial Brand Velocity Score (BVS) and introduces a straightforward way to categorise customers. Three clear categories emerge:

1. **Growers:** Those who see the brand as growing.
2. **Neutrals:** Those who see the brand as static.
3. **Decliners:** Those who see it declining.

Understanding each of these segments and how they feel about your brand will explain what is and isn't working in your brand strategy and marketing. The differences between these three categories will provide insights about who they are, how they feel and perceive your brand and your competitors, and most importantly, how to win them as customers.

The segmentation will also help with brand planning and strategy. This should focus on moving those who are Neutrals (i.e. see the brand as static) and Decliners into the Growers segment. Increasing the number of people who believe you are growing (and reducing the number of Decliners) will mean your audience is primed, receptive to your marketing messages, and ready to listen and act.

We recommend reviewing and monitoring the BVS for both your brand users and non-users separately. Typically, users score higher than non-users due to their more positive relationship with your brand. Occasionally, we see signs that some brands have exceptionally high BVS scores amongst users; this might suggest a loyal fan base or that the customer marketing is particularly effective.

It is also essential to keep an eye on competitors' performance. Ideally, brands must achieve the highest brand velocities in their competitive set to ensure growth. If your velocity is lower than most key competitors, it suggests radical action is needed to elevate your momentum. Typically, brands within a sector will be tightly clustered within a range of +10 and -10 of each other. This tight clustering is expected, as most brands will be affected by perceptions of the category, which will affect the velocity of all brands within the market.

Momentum Principle 4
Signalling Inner Confidence

Crowing about successes or making exaggerated claims may well backfire. Over the past 40 years of running focus groups, I've learned that there are some things brands shouldn't say. People don't typically like 'braggers', and whilst this may vary by culture, some messages simply don't resonate with the public, even if they are true!

In the UK, there are examples of consumer backlash when companies are felt to be too big, or making too much money – Tesco in the early noughties is a prime example of suffering from dominance, although it has successfully recovered well from this lesson.

There are several reasons why things shouldn't be said, and these are:

- **The topic or idea is socially taboo.** Most people believe the stereotype that businesses and their leaders are selfish, don't care about their customers, and only care about money and profits. People rarely talk about money publicly, and neither should brands (except to investors).
- **Magicians should never reveal their secrets.** Magicians don't show how they do magic tricks; similarly, for brands, revealing some things can destroy the magic. Secret recipes and how things are made are all part of the mystery and part of brands and life. So keep them secret.
- **Show, not tell.** Let's face it, some things don't sound good when said out aloud. Sometimes the only way to understand or feel something is through experience.

The word 'signals', which I relate to vitality, social fitness, brand fitness and altruism, was deliberately chosen to convey that these attributes need to be inferred rather than overtly shouted about. If you want to take a direct route, then social media is the best way to tell people what your brand is up to or how it is doing, but even then, tread carefully because no one likes to feel manipulated.

In most situations, you must take an indirect approach to maximise your BVS. I recommend you avoid any explicit suggestions that you are focused on growth unless it relates to your brand purpose and CSR. For example, if you have a goal to reduce poverty or raise money for charity or other good causes, then these are laudable and can be communicated overtly. But overall, it is better to be seen as growing because of your efforts to satisfy consumers and their needs.

A momentum strategy should be out of sight for your customers, and the effects of your brand should be seen, not heard. No one likes people who boast, and the same applies to brands. So, focus on signalling and leveraging the things that convey success.

Another reason why signalling is essential is because many of us are suspicious of advertising claims. Signalling is different as it bypasses the conscious brain and talks to the subconscious mind, scanning for information about the brand. Indeed, the effects of advertising are often subtle and work at a subconscious level; sometimes, we don't even realise we have seen or heard it. We all believe we have free will, so keep your momentum messages at the implicit and subconscious levels.

There are many ways of conveying the momentum signals of social fitness and vitality to your intended audience. Here are just a few examples and ideas to illustrate the signals and how to improve BVS without mentioning growth or success in your communications.

Communicating Social Signals

Social proof is heavily used in marketing today, demonstrating the quality of the product or service through reviews and ratings. Almost everyone these days uses reviews, and around half of all shoppers rate online reviews as one of their top 3 influences in their purchase decisions.

Being ubiquitous and available to everyone is an excellent way to signal popularity and keep you in front of mind – although a specific user image is usually more powerful in signalling relevance. Conveying popularity in advertising is often straightforward and can be done by showing happy people in relevant occasions.

However, using celebrities in advertising can be effective in demonstrating popularity, user imagery, occasions and situations, as well as emotions and connections. Just choose your celeb carefully to match the expectations of your audience! If you are trying to bypass user imagery (e.g., you don't want to portray a stereotype), as you have a broad demographic, then the use of fictional characters and animals can help achieve this.

Signalling Brand Vitality

Demonstrating that the brand is active and engaging with the world is one thing that is expected of all brands. To help improve your BVS, you must imbue or demonstrate the qualities of youthfulness and vitality. Enthusiasm, energy and excitement are popular youthful qualities in the Western world.

As we know, keeping the user imagery in tune with your customers is important. Remember, they like to think they are 10-20% younger than they are in most cases. If you want to target today's youth, image is paramount because none of them want to drive or wear the clothes their parents wear. So you may be wise to warn off older customers from visiting or buying your brand – otherwise, they could kill off your brand for this young audience. This can be done through a number of cumulative signals. For example, in all imagery show younger people, employ young staff, spotlight edgy fashion which might alienate them, keep fit and sizing small and less generous, focus marketing on digital channels, play louder modern music and don't provide comfy seating!

Research shows that video, film and TV typically create the strongest emotions and are often the most effective in building brands and a great way to add life and dynamism to your brand and communications.

Signalling Brand Fitness

Both social and vitality signals contribute to the overall fitness of the brand. However, some specific elements and themes can be important here. Communicating desire and wealth is important, as is conveying that the company is commercially robust and successful. Our research has shown that these signals can improve the attraction of working for a company or even encourage buying shares in the business.

Demonstrating altruism is an increasingly important element of brand image to build growth and should be included as one of the aspects of fitness. Today's consumers are more ethically focused, and supporting charities and good causes is a great way to signal a more caring aspect of the business.

Cost signalling is a way to demonstrate that a brand is thriving. Extravagance, design and aesthetics are all excellent for costly signalling, which is why some companies spend millions creating lavish adverts. Partnerships with celebrities and sponsorship of sports and entertainment events are also great ways to add kudos to your brand. For more on this, see Costly Signalling Theory on page 208.

Quality is frequently associated with added value; attention to detail often counts for a lot when signalling fitness. Conveying craftsmanship and the time and effort put into a product or service, are ways to signal cost or added value.

Momentum Principle 5
Engage Emotions

Brands aren't just rational entities. Your brand isn't simply a logo, a product, or a service – it's a connection, a personality, a story and a promise.

My experience in consumer research confirms the massive influence of emotion on brand choices and commitments. Emotion not only applies to consumer brands but is also evident in B2B decision-making— we are all human after all! As we saw in *The Trust Delusion*, positive emotions of joy and excitement increase dramatically with interest, usage and loyalty.

Brands stir emotions and can sometimes create fierce loyalty; think of the passion surrounding football teams, political parties, pop stars and entertainment brands. In today's world of personal branding, even people are brands. We connect with them on a deeper level.

Consider the outpouring of emotion when Nestle axed the Caramac bar in November 2023 after more than 60 years. Headlines like "Fans share heartbreak over discontinuation..." illustrate people's strong feelings towards a brand – and this was for one that most of us had forgotten about.

Building brand-customer connections is fundamental to marketing. This relationship-building and the loyalty it fosters are crucial factors in extending a brand's lifespan. It's an essential aspect of momentum theory – it's not just about growth but also fostering longevity and loyalty. The thing that fascinates me about momentum theory, is that the same force that helps brands grow, also helps them to keep going - they are not different phenomena.

Emotions are the lifeblood of any brand; after all, they are what make us all care about them. In the beginning, most consumers feel relatively little for the brand in question. It's only after positive exposure and experiences that strong emotions start to form. To achieve momentum, strive to make customers feel happy, confident and excited about your brand. It's all about positive energy and vitality.

Vision One measures emotional response with its 'Brand Emotion' metric – a unique tool within its Brand Equity Wheel. This question, derived from Robert Plutchik's Wheel of Emotion, explores how people feel about a brand.

Plutchik's complex model can be simplified into eight emotions: Anger, Anticipation, Disgust, Fear, Joy, Sadness, Surprise, and Trust. These can be categorised into positive (Anticipation, Joy, Surprise, Trust) and negative (Anger, Disgust, Fear, Sadness) drivers.

The 8 Primary Emotions

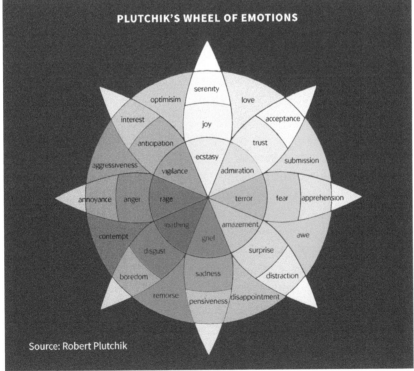

Analysing Vision One's *BrandBank*, we discovered a strong link between brand velocity and emotion.

Much of our research highlights the power of emotion for brand success and one emotion in particular – excitement! It's a key driver of the Net Promoter Score and brand loyalty, and it's strongly linked to high Brand Velocity Scores. This suggests that brands generating strong emotions create momentum and vice versa. We're further exploring how anticipation (or excitement) might play an outsized role in driving brand emotion.

Excitement and positive emotions are particularly important in helping brands grow, but they are also important drivers of advertising effectiveness and creating viral content. In his book, *Contagious – Why Things Catch On*, Jonah Berger explains what makes products, ideas, stories and news likely to spread from person to person via word of mouth and social influence. These are social currency, triggers, emotion, practical value, public and stories.

Emotions play a powerful role in how we respond to brands. Low arousal emotions like trust, contentment or sadness can make us less motivated and less likely to act. They just don't provide the same energetic spark as high-arousal emotions. To achieve high-velocity brand status, focus on cultivating awe, excitement and amusement within your brand messaging. These emotions are the fuel that stimulates memories and engagement and propels your brand forward. Negative emotions in messaging can work from time to time, such as anger, but these clearly are not associations you want to have as brand attributes.

Overall, there are some interesting parallels in Berger's book with brand velocity. In hindsight, I guess this should be expected as they both really explore different sides of the same coin, with Jonah focusing more on messaging, whilst this book is more about brand building.

Momentum Principle 6
Build a Momentum Mindset

*It is impossible to progress without change, and those
who do not change their minds cannot change anything.*

George Bernard Shaw

Leaning In and Out

Most business experts recognise the importance of innovation to every business. Thousands of brands have been left behind due to a lack of innovation or a failure to adapt to the market. Some of the most famous examples include Blockbuster, Compaq, Woolworths, Kodak, Nokia, and ToysRUs. Many retailers and high-street brands have failed to adapt to online shopping. Technology companies have also struggled, often because they have backed the wrong trends. For example, Xerox believed the future was in copying machines, and Kodak and Polaroid stuck to film rather than moving to digital. Finding ways to adapt and improve is imperative for all businesses. However, by and large, these problems can be averted by understanding consumer needs.

In his book *The Diary of a CEO*, Steven Bartlett outlines the 33 laws of business and life and makes the point that *'You Must Lean into Bizarre Behaviour'* (*Rule No. 5*). Leaning in means drawing towards, or staying in touch with trends and avoiding being left behind by technology, social or cultural shifts. In this context, Bartlett refers to the bizarre as that which is new and different initially, but might be tomorrow's new normal. CEOs and marketers miss these shifts at their peril. The opposite, 'Leaning out', is where ignorance or arrogance occurs and where business leaders falsely believe they are right and fail to pay attention to a trend or new information.

Unlike the traditional marketer's view that brands should be strong and rigid, momentum theory differs in that one half of the brand should be consistent (the brand identity) and the other half evolving (the brand velocity). They are completely different elements of a brand and should not be confused. I've often seen brands and researchers confuse the two elements – assuming that velocity characteristics such as popular, desirable and exciting are permanent and integral to the brand. In many cases they are not; they are purely symptoms of its velocity and lifecycle. They will change and will disappear when momentum is lost.

Brands need to be consistent in style and approach and have a signature that everyone should recognise. However, if you're looking to grow, this dynamic and flexible part of a brand is much more important than the rigid brand identity and assets. The fluidity is what creates momentum and gives the brand 'wiings' as Red Bull puts it.

The rate of change in the world is accelerating. Consequently, people are becoming more used to change and, ultimately, more receptive to it. It is no coincidence that brands on the stock markets around the world are getting younger and younger, nor is it any real surprise that the average age of companies in the UK is just 8.6 years. This increase in the rate of change means that brands must put more emphasis on their BVS in the future.

As the investor Martin Zwieg once said, *"The trend is your friend"* – you must go with it rather than fight it. Unfortunately, no one knows how big an idea will become, but a momentum strategy requires you to keep looking and prepare to react when the time comes. It's a bit like being a surfer and knowing which wave to catch. Numerous organisations worldwide are constantly on the lookout for and monitoring trends, and they can be a great source to help you keep ahead of the curve and be a trendsetter rather than a follower. People like brands to be edgy and bold, not just followers.

After decades of research, a renowned Stanford University psychologist, Carol Dweck, captured the idea of the power of our mindset in a book titled *Mindset: The New Psychology of Success*. She discovered that it's not just our abilities and talent that bring us success but also our approach and whether we have a fixed or growth mindset. It's a book with some inspiring stories. It offers the simple concept of fostering a love of learning and resilience, which can lead to some outstanding achievements in most walks of life. Remaining positive and open-minded, and even something as simple as changing the wording, such as 'No' to 'Not yet' can have a powerful impact on our ability to improve.

A few ideas that I have 'found and borrowed from others', to help run a business and achieve a momentum strategy are:

- **Shared vision:** Creating and sharing a vision and values with everyone – a brand can only create momentum with teamwork and collaboration. As we'll see in the next chapter, the brand purpose is a great way to help involve the customer too.
- **High energy:** From time to time, I find low energy creeping into our business, and the only way to keep it out is by promoting a high-energy business. This is where people are engaged and motivated, always seeking a positive resolution to every issue. Energy, enthusiasm and passion are the fuel that ignites us to act.
- **Without fear:** Developing a momentum mindset and willingness to try new things without fear of failure is essential. As Sir Richard Branson said, *"My attitude has always been, if you fall flat on your face, at least you're moving forward. All you have to do is get back up and try again."* According to the Harvard Business School, 80% of new products launched each year fail to meet their objectives, so it is important to research ideas thoroughly. Find a way to test and develop your ideas quickly – remember you are not representative of the person who will buy your brand.
- **Agreeableness can kill success:** Agreeableness might seem like a good thing in business, but it isn't always beneficial. The Wisdom of the Crowd theory supports this and suggests that the team should be as diverse as possible to ensure a range of perspectives and not a bunch of 'yes guys'. If you have a 'without fear' culture, then honesty and openness will prevail and better decisions will emerge.

- **Showing trust:** Leaders should encourage their team to grow, and mistakes should be allowed if others are to learn. From experience, I have found letting go with one of the hardest thing to do – but once you have done it a few times, you soon realise others can pick up the mantle.

Innovation and Brand Extensions

Let's face it, innovation is costly and often risky. Most new products fail, with estimates ranging from a high of 80% to a more moderate 50%. Nevertheless, getting innovation right is essential for many successful businesses. Doing nothing is not an option. As Albert Einstein once said, *"Insanity is doing the same thing over and over again and expecting different results."* Stagnation is the antithesis of innovation.

Our research into momentum supports this notion and highlights the role of innovation in generating a high BVS. Brands that consistently innovate are significantly more likely to be perceived as growing – those that don't are often labelled 'failures' by consumers. If you are looking to grow, then innovation should be integral to your business strategy.

In 2022, Kantar concluded that the most successful 'breakthrough brands' over-index significantly on disruption and innovation. These brands scored 20% higher than average on 'shaking things up' and 18% higher on 'leading the way'. They are also more likely to rate 'innovation' higher. These results are precisely the sort of perceptions we would expect from fast-growing brands with a high BVS. But don't assume that the biggest brands can't achieve high velocity – indeed, some of the fastest-growing brands perceptually are global giants, including the likes of Google and Tesla.

There are two schools of thought about brands. Some believe brands should remain narrowly focused and that the introduction of sub-brands, line extensions and brand extensions simply dilutes and detracts from the core brand. However, experience has shown that this thinking is flawed. Strategic brand extensions help create momentum and can strengthen brands. For example, consider Disney's move into theme parks, Virgin's expansion from records into everything from airlines to banking, and

Google's launch of the Pixel phone. These brands were already well-established before they diversified, which certainly helped, but these additions have further strengthened their overall brand presence.

Clearly, not all extensions work. Look at Coca-Cola's failed products, including New Coke (aimed to taste like Pepsi), Coca-Cola Blak (a foray into luxury coffee), and Diet Coke Plus (with various vitamins and antioxidants). While these missteps happened, they haven't damaged the overall Coca-Cola brand, which still remains dominant across the globe. The question is, if Coke hadn't tried to innovate, would it still be the dominant player it is today?

My final thought is that momentum must be a strategic priority in every C-suite or boardroom, regularly monitored against competitors. While growth can be achieved by increasing the number of 'growers' and reducing the proportion of 'decliners,' successful brands require alignment throughout the entire organisation to fully capitalise on creating positive momentum.

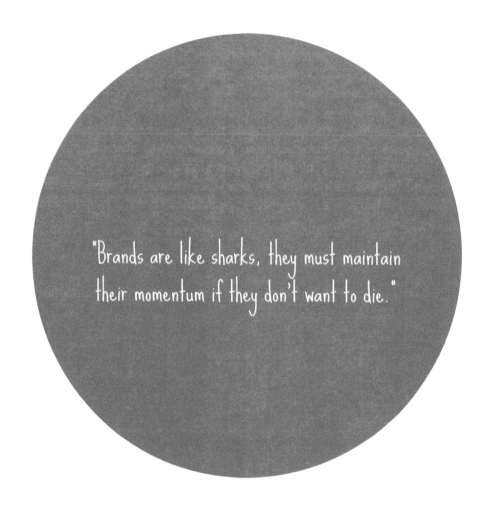

"Brands are like sharks, they must maintain their momentum if they don't want to die."

Chapter VIII

Planning for Momentum

*All our dreams can come true; if we have
the courage to pursue them.*

Walt Disney

I'm a great believer that a brand strategy should, at the very least, be exciting. If you're not excited by your goal or vision, how can you expect others to follow it? All your goals and ambitions are reflected in your brand and marketing statements. So, your purpose, vision, mission, positioning and promises should all work together to create a clear and coherent story or dream for the future.

If you are looking for a brand and marketing strategy that will gain the support of any CEO, focusing it on growth and maximising your BVS is surely the way to go. Before we look at building your strategy in more detail, here is a brief explanation of the key components of the overall strategy and how you can weave in brand momentum.

By now, you have probably come to appreciate that brands aren't just static and that they shouldn't change or evolve – they must grow. Did you know some sharks will die if they stop moving? The great white shark, whale shark, hammerhead and mako sharks would all suffocate without forward motion or a strong current flowing towards their mouths – brands are no different and must continue moving to survive.

"Keep my momentum going and things will go swimmingly."

This chapter focuses on the brand, creating your brand vision and mission, and incorporating a momentum philosophy. We'll examine how some of the world's iconic brands do it and what underpins their success.

Planning Your Brand's Future

Brand purpose is your brand's superpower.
Karen Bailey

Purpose – Why Your Brand Exists

It's inspiring to see brands connect with customers by emphasising purpose beyond profit. This shift aligns with customers increasingly seeking brands that represent something more profound. Businesses focused less on profits and more on consumers are finding this new approach brings extra rewards.

A brand's purpose refers to its reason for existing, similar to a mission statement. However, today, purpose often incorporates a socially conscious, altruistic approach. At its core, assuming it is authentic, a brand purpose explains how the brand benefits society. This outward-facing, customer-centric perspective is key to a momentum-focused strategy – we all appreciate kindness, after all.

Coca-Cola's global water stewardship efforts exemplify a brand purpose in action. A powerful purpose clearly states why the brand exists and benefits everyone, not just the company. It should:

* Add value for customers and society
* Differentiate your brand from the competition
* Provide clarity and foster a strong corporate culture where employees rally around and embrace a shared goal.

Our research into the drivers of BVS suggests that high-velocity brands are more likely to be seen as providing a positive social impact. This idea of doing good was 150% more likely to be associated with growing brands than declining brands. There is growing evidence that people are attracted more towards brands that demonstrate their Corporate Social Responsibility (CSR) credentials. Indeed, in today's world, it's not good enough just to have a purpose, but brands must now differentiate themselves through purpose.

Previously, the 'doing good' space was the domain of charities and non-profit organisations, but well-known brands in this space include purpose-focused brands such as Patagonia, which seeks to operate in ways that minimise environmental impact. Beyond Meat seeks to address four growing global issues: human health, climate change, constraints on natural resources, and animal welfare.

To be an effective momentum-based strategy, the purpose should be transformative and progressive. It needs to create a sense of change with no endpoint in sight but rather a continuous journey towards a better future. If there is an endpoint when people realise this has been achieved, there is no longer a reason for people to buy the brand or for it to exist.

> Tesla: *"To accelerate the world's transition to sustainable energy,"* evokes powerful change while acknowledging the long journey ahead. This sense of momentum is crucial.

> Coca-Cola: *"To refresh the world. To inspire moments of optimism and happiness, creating a positive impact in the world."* Here again, the focus is on transformation and has no obvious endpoint.

> Nike: *"To bring innovation and inspiration to every athlete in the world – If you have a body, then you're an athlete."* Reaching everyone is ultimately the endgame of a momentum strategy, and Nike's vision is eternal.

In summary, a brand purpose should use active words to explain why you do what you do for the world and the benefits it might bring. It should be short, less than 20 words, emotional, and perpetual without an end in sight.

Vision Statement – The Brand's Future

The vision statement is short, typically one sentence, and outlines the ambitions and future goals of your brand, albeit more commercially focused. The purpose and vision should be aligned to create a consistent story.

As we can see from the examples below, the vision is quite broad and not too prescriptive about a single market, giving the brand space to move in the future.

> Starbucks: *"To establish Starbucks as the premier purveyor of the finest coffee in the world while maintaining our uncompromising principles while we grow."* Note the inclusion of the word "grow" fits well with a momentum strategy!

> Amazon: *"To be Earth's most customer-centric company, where customers can find and discover anything they might want to buy online."* Again, the vision is far-reaching and focused on touching everyone across the globe.

> Tesco: *"Serving Britain's shoppers a little better every day. No matter how you shop with us, we always want to provide you with the best possible experience."* This vision fits well with a momentum strategy, as it gives the sense that there is an ongoing journey of improvement and growth.

The vision is arguably the most important aspect of a momentum strategy, as it focuses on the future and moving the company (and the world) forward. Unlike the purpose, it should focus on the market or category and the brand's future position. Ideally, it should include elements from either or both the social and brand energies. If this is not a public-facing statement, then it can include momentum and BVS references.

One final thing to say about purpose and vision is that they need to be shared somehow with the public to have an impact and create a common goal. Don't just talk about your brand, share stories about the bigger picture and the progress the world is making towards your vision for a better world.

A Word about Values

So, whilst Brand Purpose and Altruism are important in helping brands grow, I am less convinced about brand values and believe they are better suited to internal (rather than external) communications.

For example, here are three companies' brand values I found online at random:

> Pizza Hut: We're honest, transparent, and committed to doing what's best for our customers and our company. We are guided by solid moral compasses and constantly push ourselves to be our best.

> Allianz Care: Customer & Market Excellence, Collaborative Leadership, Trust and Entrepreneurship.

> Colgate: By living our Colgate Values of Caring, Inclusive and Courageous, we create a culture in which people act as a team, working together toward common goals.

Focus on Promises rather than Values

Recent research suggests that promises can be more effective. Committing to customers is stronger than just stating values; brands should move in this direction.

This was illustrated in Mimi Turner's Nudgestock 2023 presentation, 'Every Product Needs a Promise'. She argues that clear promises to customers are essential for successful marketing and lead to increased brand health, market share and long-term sales growth. Examples include BT's unbreakable wi-fi, Snickers' satisfaction guarantee, and successful campaigns built on these promises. The results of Turner's investigation into over 2000 campaigns showed that there was a 48%

greater likelihood of increasing brand health when you make a promise to the customer.

Using WARC's extensive library of award-winning-campaigns, the research shows that campaigns with a promise are more likely to create brand health improvements. However, it is perhaps no surprise that promises are less likely to create buzz (i.e. a social media or PR impact) as promises tend to focus on brand building rather than achieving press coverage. This makes brand promises ideal for those looking to create a momentum strategy.

A brand promise should be simple, credible, memorable, and focused on your audience's needs and wants. Try to make your promises appeal to emotions and/or be tied to action or responsibility.

McDonald's has three key promises: Consistency, Speed, and Fun. These are great values, but the promise makes them more special. Perhaps most important is the consistent quality of their food, served quickly across the globe. The other promises – Speed (e.g., drive-through) and Fun (e.g., kids' meals) – are inherent in their offering.

Tesco also has three promises centred around the notion that 'No one tries harder for customers': to understand customers, to be the first to meet their needs and to act responsibly for communities. I particularly like the second promise, which indicates agility, while the first and third confirm the brand's customer-centric focus, which I believe in itself is also a form of altruism.

Crafting a Brand Positioning Statement

Brand owners should also include a well crafted Brand Positioning Statement for their brand and marketing plans. A brand positioning statement showcases your unique value and explains why customers should choose you over the competition. It should balance aspiration and reality. When creating one, consider:

- Who is your ideal target market?
- What is your product/service offering?

- What is the greatest benefit and impact of your offering?
- What proof do you have of the benefit and impact?
- What emotional aspects does your brand have?

Burger King's 'Have it Your Way' campaign perfectly summarises their strategy and positioning. It implies fresh, made-to-order meals, contrasting them with boring, standardised fast food. Their updated 'You Rule' campaign further emphasises customer empowerment.

When considering your momentum strategy, ensure you keep your target market age profile and user image well aligned - and do not be tempted to let your user imagery age with time.

Ensuring your product is relevant and offers a wide range of benefits and usage occasions is essential to appeal to the broadest audience.

Whilst any form of evidence can be helpful in making your brand more compelling, don't forget Social Proof and shaping the WorldView are critical.

In most markets, emotions are key to creating momentum, where consumers value Joy and Excitement above most other feelings and emotions.

A Momentum Dashboard

Today, most CMOs use a range of metrics to determine the success of their strategy. I believe most strategies should be single-minded, for this reason dashboards and metrics should all be focused on achieving the overall goal. They should also work harmoniously, all support the fundamental goal. So, for anyone looking to achieve a momentum-based strategy, I believe the most important brand and marketing KPIs can be distilled down to five key metrics.

5 Key Metrics: Awareness, Emotion, Mass, BVS & Momentum

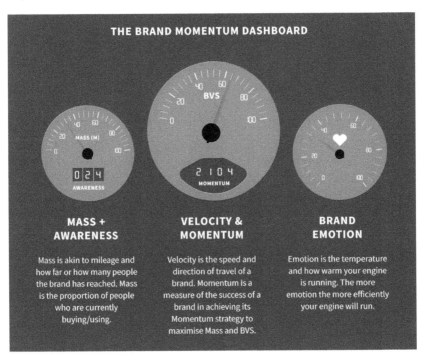

THE BRAND MOMENTUM DASHBOARD

MASS + AWARENESS

Mass is akin to mileage and how far or how many people the brand has reached. Mass is the proportion of people who are currently buying/using.

VELOCITY & MOMENTUM

Velocity is the speed and direction of travel of a brand. Momentum is a measure of the success of a brand in achieving its Momentum strategy to maximise Mass and BVS.

BRAND EMOTION

Emotion is the temperature and how warm your engine is running. The more emotion the more efficiently your engine will run.

Multiple metrics are useful from a diagnostic point of view, but as illustrated above, the most important groups of measurement are Brand Awareness or similar salience metrics (e.g., mental availability), Mass, Brand Emotion, and finally, BVS and Momentum metrics. These are just like the mileage, speedometer and temperature gauges in a car, giving vital clues about how the vehicle is running.

Briefly, I believe these are important for the following reasons:

1. Brand Awareness and other brand salience measures are important, they provide clues as to how many people within your target market have been reached. Your ultimate aim is to stay at the top of your target audience's minds. This takes years, but as you grow, it will become cheaper and easier with time.

   Brand awareness and mass are interdependent; the more people are aware of your brand, the more customers you are likely to have. So, with any increase in awareness, you should experience a rise in the number of customers, too. However, it's important to remember that velocity is your driving force for growth, not awareness, which is simply the outcome of marketing and momentum.

2. Emotion is like the engine's temperature and relates to your target audience's emotional warmth. As we have seen, emotion is one of the most potent human characteristics that drives feelings and actions. This is true of brands; momentum and repeat sales are highly unlikely without emotion. Emotion is also at the heart of positive word of mouth, central to creating momentum and encouraging people to act.

3. We have already covered brand velocity and momentum in detail. However, there are some important ways to consider these when deciding what action to take. Using a momentum strategy is quite straightforward, and to monitor it, you simply need the right measurements and to understand how your competitors perform on the same metrics. A successful momentum strategy simply means that you need a strong BVS to see increases in penetration (number of users each year). If you are not seeing your mass increase, then action is required.

Brand Momentum Quadrant Analysis

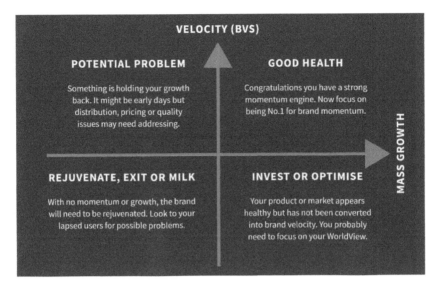

As shown above, brands simply need to focus on getting the brand to sit in the top right quadrant and then focus on the elements or issues holding it back. Ideally, the positioning within this top-right quadrant would be higher and further right than any rivals.

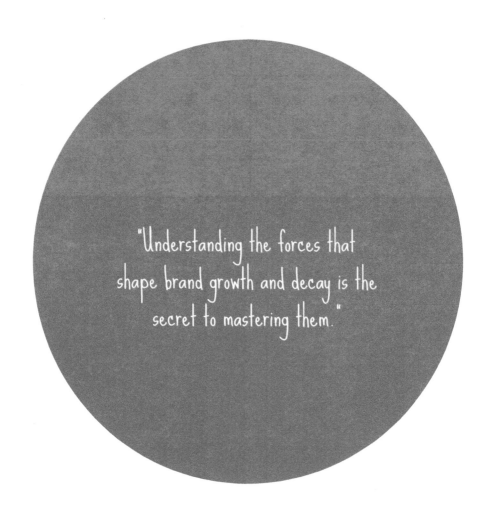

"Understanding the forces that shape brand growth and decay is the secret to mastering them."

Chapter IX
Driving Momentum
Through Advertising

Good advertising does not just circulate information.
It penetrates the public mind with desires and belief.

Leo Burnett

Advertising is central to creating momentum. Brands which advertise are likely to be seen as growing. Moreover, research shows that people are more attentive to brands with velocity. Additionally, mass is also one of the biggest drivers of advertising ROI. Momentum ultimately leads to additional growth and more effective marketing.

Once you have a strategy for your brand, you will need to focus on how to achieve it. Given that a momentum strategy is about the battle for people's minds, we will explore how to achieve momentum through advertising and marketing.

The role of advertising is well known and is important to brands and those looking to grow their customers and increase revenues for the following key reasons:

1. **Increases awareness and familiarity:** Advertising helps to improve a brand's visibility, raising brand awareness and creating familiarity and velocity.
2. **Builds identity:** Advertising can help establish and reinforce brand identity, signalling vitality, fitness and social aspects to create a more compelling brand.
3. **Establishes emotional connections:** Advertising creates emotional connections between consumers and brands, often leading to increased empathy, loyalty and brand advocacy.
4. **Creates brand velocity:** Advertising makes brands more attractive. It helps reduce the proportion of people who find them unattractive, removes barriers and eliminates friction. The impact of advertising on BVS and overall brand momentum is significant.

Extensive research into advertising effectiveness indicates that the most significant factors are the size of the advertising budget and the range of media[12]. Our own consumer research shows that perceptions of growing and declining brands are significantly affected by advertising and the 'noise' brands generate.

Impact of Media on Brand Velocity

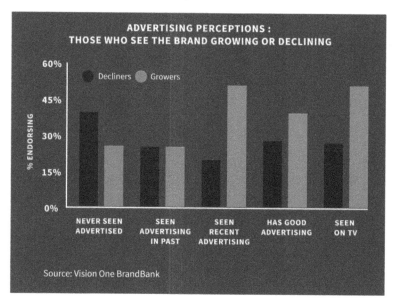

As illustrated above, the brands thought to be growing were much more likely to have advertised recently, and were more likely to have been on TV or YouTube. Declining brands were more likely to have never been seen to advertise. Past advertising has some impact (i.e. better than no advertising), and the benefit of recent advertising awareness is clear to see. Interestingly, in the consumer's eyes, good advertising doesn't seem so important in driving growth. So, whether someone thinks the advertising is good or not doesn't appear as important as the advertising itself in growing BVS. The process of advertising in itself appears to create a significant uplift in your BVS, regardless of the message.

Media choice does appear important in driving BVS, with TV and video (e.g., YouTube) leading the way. According to numerous studies[13], despite increased costs and reduced reach in the UK in recent years, TV (including on-demand), has consistently remained the most effective way to build a brand. It creates much more significant business effects than other media. This includes ROI, market share gains, profitability, consumer spend, loyalty, etc. As we can see in the table, it is also an excellent way to create momentum.

Size Matters (Mass)

As we know, the size of a brand is a fundamental part of brand momentum theory. However, brand size has also been found to be the most influential factor in shaping the return on investment, profitability and overall effectiveness of advertising. As we're about to discover in the table below, it has even been proven to outstrip the creative element of advertising.

Mark Ritson is a brand consultant with a PhD in Marketing from Lancaster University and was previously a marketing professor at London Business School. Today, he is recognised as one of the world's leading marketing consultants. In 2019, along with MBA students, he dived deep into 50 years and a total of 5,900 entries to the Effie Awards to help answer what drives effective advertising and marketing campaigns. All the award entries were scored in terms of their effectiveness and, where possible, coded on various elements. For example, 10th on his list is market research, which highlighted that papers that appeared to have little or no research performed worse than those that used some or a lot of research.

At the event organised by ThinkTV in 2019[14], Ritson gave his view based on the analysis of the ten most important factors that drive effectiveness. Top of this list was the brand's size (e.g., mass), the most influential factor in driving effectiveness. It was suggested that this was because large brands have developed – among other things – pre-existing mental structures, distribution, products and loyalty.

Mark Ritson's Effectiveness Top 10[15]

1. **Brand size**
2. **Creativity**
3. **Brand 'codes' (e.g., Distinctive assets)**
4. **Excess share of voice**
5. **Balancing mass and targeted marketing**
6. **Long- and short-term communications**
7. **Multichannel mix**
8. **Realistic differentiation**
9. **Set meaningful strategic objectives**
10. **(Some) Market research**

I believe the importance of brand size is easy to explain as larger brands have more users and already built a connection with most people. Our advertising testing and evaluation system, 'AdProbe,' is used to test near- or fully-finished executions; we find that buyers and users of a brand are much more receptive to the brand's advertising (vs. non-users). The biggest brands will always have the most users, and due to this priming, advertising will often attract more sales from existing customers, including lighter and less loyal customers, rather than totally new users.

The importance of brand size was highlighted through econometric analysis of individual campaigns by Paul Dyson, co-founder of Accelero.[16] See the illustration below.

So, unfortunately, until brands have 'made it' on the journey to becoming a household name, smaller brands will often need to invest more heavily in advertising to achieve growth. In contrast, larger brands must spend relatively less to maintain their share. However, smaller brands in high-value categories (e.g., travel, subscription, cars, and finance) could readily achieve increased turnover and a strong ROI.

The Power of Brand Size on ROI

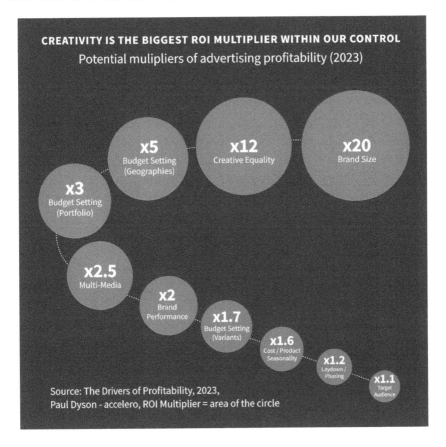

Advertising Spend and Share of Voice Drives Growth

It won't come as any surprise to say that brands that spend more on marketing will outperform those that don't and that media spending is the main driver of brand growth.

Share of Voice (SOV), or put another way, the share of market advertising, shows a key relationship with growth. Research from the IPA and Nielsen in 2019 indicated that a brand increasing its share of voice typically saw an increase in total market share.[17] The gains made by one brand can also result in significant share losses for competitors. Generally, if you can afford it, your SOV should exceed its market share to achieve growth.

While researching SOV, I found some fascinating work in WARC by Robert Brittain and Peter Field, from 2021, titled 'To ESOV and Beyond'.[18] As illustrated below, Excess Share Of Voice (ESOV) impacts brand health and mental availability. Not only did it significantly impact long-term market share growth, but it also did well on short-term share gains. However, other key benefits are the strengthening of pricing, the acquisition of new customers, customer retention and the improvement of profitability – these sound just like what we would expect from a brand achieving momentum and increasing its BVS.

The Importance of Excess Share of Voice

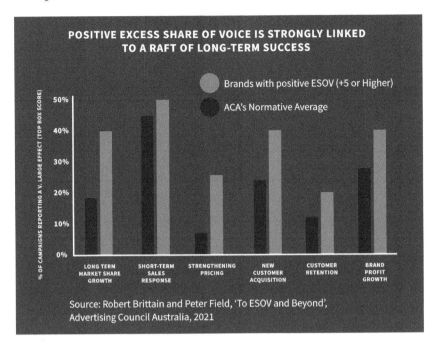

POSITIVE EXCESS SHARE OF VOICE IS STRONGLY LINKED TO A RAFT OF LONG-TERM SUCCESS

Source: Robert Brittain and Peter Field, 'To ESOV and Beyond', Advertising Council Australia, 2021

Whilst I recognise that every brand's budget and financial strength differ in every market, this principle provides a level of investment brands should strive for. The general rule of thumb recommended for advertising spend is 5% to 10% of turnover. However, the good news is that campaign success isn't just about how much you spend. Creative quality is the second most important after media investment.

The Power of Brand Building

*A product can be quickly outdated, but
a successful brand is timeless.*

Stephen King, best-selling author

**Brand-building advertising is more effective than
activation in the long-term, and advertising that seeks
to grow new customers is the most effective strategy.
Combined with a continuous or drip campaign, this
makes for the ideal momentum-building strategy.**

As you will recall, in the Chapter III section Adopting an Acquisition Strategy, I highlighted the two types of marketing or ways advertising can work: either short-term activation or longer-term brand building. Short-term advertising is focused on people in the market, and this might include a limited-time discount or offer to drive immediate sign-ups. Conversely, a brand-building campaign for a running shoe company could focus on inspirational stories of how their footwear can benefit the wider public, leading to long-term brand affinity and increased sales in the future.

Short-term advertising looks to make an immediate impact, and this type of marketing is sometimes referred to as 'performance marketing' or 'sales activation'. It focuses on making a sale or taking immediate action, such as visiting a website or downloading from the web, etc. These types of short-term marketing tend to involve behavioural nudges designed to get an immediate reaction or decision. Short-term advertising techniques, such as 'Buy One, Get One' promotions often seen in supermarkets, create a sense of urgency but are unlikely to build long-term brand loyalty.

Short-term advertising attempts to create a sense of urgency (e.g., sales ending soon, the last few remaining, and limited-time offers (LTOs), etc). These are outside this book's scope as they rarely drive momentum or help with brand-building. But, please note that brand-building advertising still needs to create some short-term effects to be effective – so look for a combination of both (i.e. instil some desire to act). Even a powerful brand-building campaign for a luxury car might include a limited-time financing offer to incentivise immediate action.

On the other hand, brand-building advertising attempts to create longer-lasting effects and growth – which could be viewed as momentum (i.e. continuous growth). In some cases, successful brand-building campaigns achieve exponential rather than linear growth. The visual illustrates the conceptual difference between short-term advertising effects versus long-term brand building. As you can see, there are no real long-term benefits from a short-term approach, which only provides short-term gains.

Brand Building Is More Effective Long Term

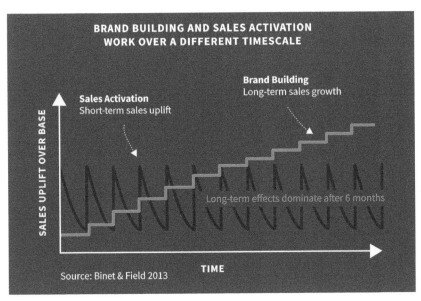

BRAND BUILDING AND SALES ACTIVATION
WORK OVER A DIFFERENT TIMESCALE

Brand Building
Long-term sales growth

Sales Activation
Short-term sales uplift

SALES UPLIFT OVER BASE

Long-term effects dominate after 6 months

TIME

Source: Binet & Field 2013

While brand building still has smaller short-term spikes, it has a cumulative effect. This phenomenon is precisely what we would expect momentum to achieve. In essence, each wave of advertising increases the BVS, so a brand sees cumulative growth where it returns to a higher base level rather than quickly returning to the same levels pre-advertising. In other words, brand building means that more people are buying at the end of the advertising period for a sustained period. In reality, advertising can be a mix of both of these effects, but analysis of effectiveness research case studies concludes that brand building is the most cost-effective in the long term.

As we know, momentum-based marketing needs to focus on customer acquisition, by winning new buyers and re-engaging lapsed customers. Here's the good news. There is considerable evidence to suggest that campaigns focusing on penetration growth (i.e. gaining more new customers) are most effective in creating large sales effects for a brand.

In their *Marketing Effectiveness in the Digital Era* (2007),[19] Les Binet and Peter Field highlighted that very large advertising effects are most commonly achieved through campaigns that target penetration growth rather than either loyalty only or a combination of both loyalty and penetration. Their compelling report, *'The Long and the Short of It'* (2012)[20], examined the business effects of 1,000 advertising campaigns from over 30 years of IPA effectiveness data.

For many, this report changed the shape and understanding of how advertising works, including myself, and heralded a new evidence-based approach to advertising because:

- Short- and long-term advertising effects work differently; short-term metrics, especially direct response rates, may not accurately guide long-term success.

- Long-term investment in advertising delivers double the profit of a short-term approach.

- Brands targeting the whole market achieve three times as many large business effects as those focusing on existing customers. The current thinking is that you should target everyone (i.e. users and non-users).

- Advertisers need a combination of long-term investment in brand-building and short-term, direct methods that stimulate sales.

The report confirmed much of the work Vision One has been conducting on the impact of emotional advertising suggested it is twice as efficient and profitable as rational advertising. It has been long-established that creativity is important for effective advertising, and Nielsen's 2006 Project Apollo found that 65% of brands' sales lift came from the creative treatment. Creativity was followed by reach (22%) and brand attributes (15%).

So, in a nutshell, extensive advertising evaluation concludes that the most effective advertising is focused on brand building, attracting new customers and emotion. The general rule of thumb for marketing spend seems to be 60% or more on brand building and 40% or less on short-term marketing.

However, most companies don't reach this 60% level. So why is this? My belief, from the research amongst CMOs is that various factors are at play:

1. Results can take 1-2 years or more for cumulative effects to show, which may be too long for some businesses and CMOs looking to make a mark. (Short-term sales effects are much easier to spot and attribute to advertising.)
2. Brand-building campaigns will potentially show fewer short-term uplifts, so they may be considered a failure before giving the campaign time to achieve long-term growth.
3. Existing brand tracking methods might not be sensitive to, or focused on, the metrics that can predict long-term growth (e.g., BVS and momentum). Therefore, campaign effects are not accurately evaluated, which could lead to a premature change in strategy.

Drip or Burst?

In my formative client-side years, I still remember the debates we used to have over whether a burst (high impact) or drip (steady flow) campaign was best. I would argue that if you were going for a momentum-based strategy, then a drip or continuous approach would be more effective.

In an ideal world, as already mentioned, you would be outspending your competitors (i.e. ESOV). In addition, I believe you would aim for continuous or drip advertising to help keep the brand in mind and provide ongoing signalling that the brand is active. This idea was backed up by Phil Shaw in *Admap* magazine in December 2014[21], with ten pieces of evidence-based learning from Ipsos' tracking and testing database, which concluded that continuous or pulsed campaigns are better than on/off.

However, it might differ for young/small brands and those new to TV. In 2019, Paul Dyson from Data2Decisions (WARC 2019)[22] analysed 78 small brands to understand the value of TV to smaller brands and concluded that payback was quick and that these small brands should focus on a 'burst' strategy with shorter ads (rather than a 'drip' campaign), concentrating on creating brand awareness.

The Art of Signalling

A flower is a weed with an advertising budget

Rory Sutherland

Signalling is the art of non-verbal communication and an important part of creating momentum. It's the subliminal messages that can stick to a brand, and these can be essential to achieving momentum. Flowers and weeds are the same thing – they are merely differentiated by a matter of taste.

As we already know, momentum isn't something you can talk directly to your customers about; it's something they must feel and gather for themselves. So, whilst your creative advertising can impact the messages it conveys, so can your media choices.

Whilst researching for this book, I came across an excellent paper titled 'Signalling Success, (House51/Thinkbox, 2020),[23] which was thought to be the first-known UK research dedicated to the behavioural science principles of 'Costly Signalling Theory' (CST). The principle of 'costly signalling' suggests that the perceived cost and scale of an advertising channel (e.g., TV vs radio etc) translates into improved brand perceptions in the eyes of the consumer.

Costly Signalling Theory (CST) Explained

CST was developed by an evolutionary biologist named Amotz Zahavi to explain the extravagances we see across the natural world. Rory Sutherland's quote above is one of my all-time favourites, highlighting the idea that if all flowers looked the same, they would have no competitive advantage over the other flowers. So, in nature, costly signalling serves as a cue to instil trust between the signaller and observer. For example, the ornate plumage of exotic birds (e.g., peacocks, parrots) or amazing colours of tropical fish (e.g., clownfish, mandarinfish).

In a business and marketing sense, costly signalling is a form of communication requiring extra effort/difficulty or creative magic. It can be achieved through physical and psychological means, such as financial expense (e.g., advertising or shop displays), creativity/aesthetics (e.g., distinctive brand assets, stunning or clever advertising), meticulous craftsmanship and extravagance, or even honesty.

The CST research used an innovative approach influenced by academic research conducted at Duke and Stanford universities in the United States. The survey was conducted amongst 3,600 people in the UK and covered TV, newspapers, magazines, radio, social media and video-sharing sites. The clever part was that each participant was exposed to a depiction of a fictional brand, provided with a concise overview of the brand, and given a brief outline of its launch advertising campaign. Only the medium in the campaign being used was varied, to ensure any emerging differences could be isolated and explained by the media channel and nothing else.

Surprisingly, the first thing that excited me about the article was an initial literature review by Richard Shotton, which concluded that two main kinds of signals were key to advertising sales generation. It claimed that advertising drives fitness and social signals:

1. Fitness signals' image attributes of quality, financial strength and confidence.
2. Social signals' attributes being well-known, popular and successful.

This was exciting because these two signals appear to closely mirror the characteristics we associate with brand velocity – which were key aspects shaping the public's WorldView of brands. In other words, it supports the notion that advertising and the selected media channels are likely to be key drivers of BVS and brand momentum.

Their research findings were also interesting and demonstrated that TV advertising drove the strongest fitness and social signals (aka momentum), whilst social media and video-sharing sites had the lowest. The research also identified that TV, radio and magazines were perceived to be the most trusted.

TV & Paid Media Create Velocity (Social & Brand Fitness Signals)

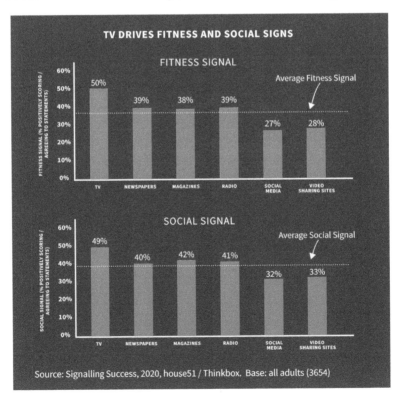

Beyond media channels, other forms of marketing will be useful to marketers looking to build their brands using some of the principles of CST. These include:

1. Extravagant marketing

Here, we are talking about embellishments that go beyond the norm. Christmas is often a time when we see many brands pushing the boat out with more extravagant advertising, amazing in-store decor, gift-wrapping services, etc. Luxury brands are often focused on this type of marketing – you only need to look down shop windows at Christmas along New Bond Street in London's West End or the Christmas tree in Galeries Lafayette in Paris. Perhaps one of the best-known exponents of CST is Disney and the way they bring their films and characters to life.

2. Sponsorships and Partnerships

Sponsorship can be a great way to build momentum by aligning with the right partners. One of the key benefits of a sponsorship is that the popularity or image of the partner (e.g., a TV programme) is passed over to the sponsor. Sponsorships can use CST by partnering with high-status partners with a high perceived cost. Some brands, like Red Bull, have chosen to go beyond sponsoring and even creating their own F1 racing team.

So, when building your momentum strategy, it is important to consider your media channels and their perceived status. If budget allows, then TV and traditional media routes are likely to offer vital contributions that social and other digital media cannot generate.

BVS Through Advertising

Advertising is about more than just driving immediate sales. It builds familiarity, shapes brand image, and fosters emotional connections. Most significantly, advertising generates momentum. Studies show that people are more likely to buy from brands they see as growing and successful.

Analysis of creative and effective ideas from WARC's *Health of Creativity Report* in 2021 showed that over half (54%) of the top campaigns used emotion as a creative strategy. If this isn't enough evidence for the power of emotion, in the same year, at the 2020 edition of the biennial IPA Effectiveness Awards, almost three-quarters (74%) of winners used emotion as their strategy.

In the report, emotion was followed by sustainability/responsibility (which can be interpreted as brand purpose or altruism). In third place, in with a bullet, was 'user-generated content or participation'. Since 2021, growth in this has been exponential, encouraging for those seeking a cost-effective route for creating success.

Over the years, through our studies in advertising effectiveness, we have created a few ground rules for creating successful advertising and a higher BVS. I call these loosely the five M's: Modern, Morality, eMotion, aMusement and Memorable.

1. **Modern (Being Topical and Relevant)**
   Marketers constantly seek emerging trends to give their brand a lift. While this is key to momentum, brands must also embody growth characteristics, like energy and excitement, to create the right environment for expansion. Most messages and new information have a sell-by date, so it's important to keep messages fresh and exciting.

2. **Morality (Doing the right thing; overcoming adversity; showing benevolence and love)**

   The recent shift towards brand purpose explains why sustainability and responsibility have become major advertising themes. The underlying concept of good vs. evil, or overcoming adversity, taps into our moral compasses and is essential for compelling storytelling. After all, who doesn't like a happy ending?

3. **eMotion (Uplifting and positive)**

   As we have stated, emotion is a widely used strategy in award-winning advertising. Powerful ads often evoke strong emotional reactions. All emotions, even sadness on occasion, are helpful. However, if you are looking to improve velocity, then creating excitement for the brand is most important.

4. **aMusement (Fun and vitality)**

   While humour might seem like a 'cheap trick', it's an important part of many brands' toolkits. Through the lens of momentum, humour conveys vitality and keeps the brand interesting and youthful.

5. **Memorable**

   Research on advertising effectiveness has shown that people often forget or misidentify advertisers. Even immediately after an advert is shown to people in a survey, they do not always correctly recall the brand name. Therefore, distinctiveness, strong branding and ensuring consumers remember your ad, are all crucial. Long-running campaigns spanning several years, often produce some of the best results.

Spreading the Word

Word of mouth is the primary factor behind 20 per cent to 50 per cent of all purchasing decisions.

Jonah Berger

While media plays a significant role in creating momentum, it's widely acknowledged that creative ideas and execution are the most important factors in determining success. The old adage 'It's not what you do, but how you do it' truly applies to all forms of marketing, not just advertising. Here, we'll briefly explore how to improve the effectiveness of marketing creativity, particularly in delivering momentum. Remember that momentum-based marketing aims to create and enhance the WorldView and MyView perceptions and experiences of brands.

Brands building their WorldView and their purpose appear to be performing well, as do those reflecting contemporary social stories. Promoting these qualities appears beneficial and can create highly effective advertising. For example, I recently saw a headline about advertising effectiveness, suggesting that advertising depicting women more positively and in an inspiring way, was more likely to achieve higher purchase consideration and perceived brand value.

Once adjusted for a brand's size, differences between brands are often subtle and simply slight variations from the category average. But what we do see, is that brand momentum explains many of the differences we think exist between brands. This is why you'll rarely find a declining brand possessing very positive image qualities.

We often associate advertising with funny mishaps, dramatic images, heartwarming stories, catchy or annoying jingles, straplines, and even celebrities. Advertising typically aims to be memorable and spur us into action. It's important to remember that in our busy, distracted lives, people aren't always engaged until you capture their attention.

As researchers, we often help brands develop and improve their advertising and marketing communications by examining public reactions to messaging and tone. Some years ago, we developed a new approach for evaluating advertising by looking at award-winning advertising from ad effectiveness awards. The pre-testing system is called AdProbe. It can test any form of marketing, from straplines to TV ads.

In the digital age, word of mouth has become more important to businesses looking to maximise the impact of any marketing investment. Reverting to Jonah Berger's book, *Contagious*, I mentioned that he identified six steps to creating virality: social currency, triggers, emotion, practical value, public, and stories.

These days, virality is often the difference between average and great advertising; essentially, it multiplies the impact by getting people to relay the message for you. However, more importantly, some of these factors that drive word of mouth also relate directly to growth and increasing brand velocity. In many ways, BVS and creating buzz, share the same traits. For example:

- **High arousal emotions get us to act.** Brands with a high BVS are exciting, and advertising is excellent for creating the right emotions – the most important are Awe, Excitement, Surprise, Amusement and Humour. Avoid focusing on low-energy emotions such as contentment, sadness and trust, as these are less likely to be transferred into momentum or be talked about, although they can work in very specific situations.

- **Practical value.** Practical value is about helping others (altruism) by sharing how a product might help the recipient save time or money. Advertising often focuses on trying to convey the benefits and features. As we have already seen, brands that are thought to be altruistic or make promises, are much more likely to achieve a higher BVS.

- **Being remarkable.** Remarkable things are unusual, extraordinary, or worthy of notice or attention. Something can be remarkable because it is novel, surprising, extreme, or just plain interesting. And these are the things we like to share. Similarly, for greater brand velocity, as mentioned earlier, you need to be distinct. The history of advertising is littered with great examples – Three's 'Dancing Pony', Kit Kat's 'Pandas', even Smash's classic 'Aliens' (for the older reader!), Cadbury's 'Gorilla' or Haribou's 'Inner Child'.

As we saw earlier, social proof is a big factor in creating velocity, and it's the same with viral marketing. Making your brand highly visible, such as the Movember Foundation and seeing men grow their facial hair in November or, more simply, the 'Bags for Life' that you now see in most stores, helps perpetuate the brand. However, seeing people use or enjoy a product in advertising is also very powerful.

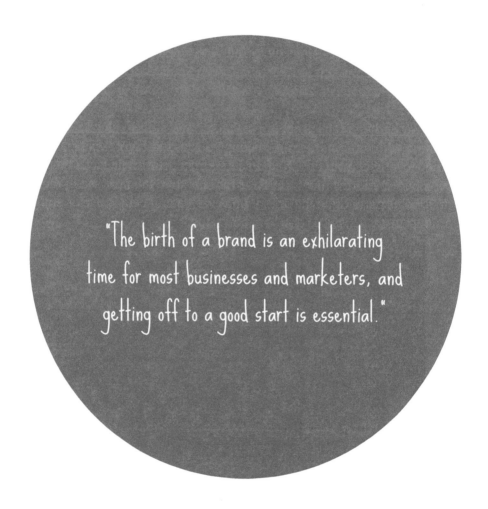

"The birth of a brand is an exhilarating time for most businesses and marketers, and getting off to a good start is essential."

Chapter X

Momentum on a Shoestring

A 'startup' is a company that is confused about
1. What its product is.
2. Who its customers are.
3. How to make money.

Dave McClure, 500Startups co-founder

This book was always intended for businesses of all sizes and backgrounds. This chapter, therefore, narrows the focus to help small businesses and start-ups begin their journey towards momentum.

Twenty-five years ago, I started my own business with very little knowledge. Reflecting on that experience, I have realised just how little I knew. While I can only share some things in one chapter, here are a few tips tailored to build momentum in start-ups and small businesses, especially those on a tight budget.

Unfortunately, momentum requires an investment in marketing – both time and money. This makes comprehensive momentum strategies better suited for larger businesses. However, the core principles are absolutely transferable! A few years ago, I had the pleasure of presenting a brand strategy to TechItalia, a London business incubator. The start-up founders particularly appreciated learning how established brands think and operate. I hope that you gain similar insights from this book.

Business experts often tell you to focus on adaptability, innovation, strong relationships, financial prudence, technology, building a great team around you, and a lot of perseverance. While this advice is sound, it won't matter if you're not impacting how potential customers think and feel about your brand. Why? Because brands exist in the minds of consumers, and consumers ultimately care most about their own needs.

Therefore, the most essential step is putting the customer at the heart of your business. Focus on understanding their wants and how you'll deliver solutions. Your core objective should be making customers care about you. This will undeniably require allocating a significant portion of your budget towards building awareness and telling your brand's story.

At Vision One, we frequently field inquiries from start-ups seeking research to validate their ideas. While we're always eager to help, we occasionally turn projects away when the ideas lack clear purpose or adequate planning. Unfortunately, many entrepreneurs believe their ideas are unique yet offer no genuine differentiation for the customer. Truly groundbreaking concepts only come along once or twice a year.

A growth mindset is indeed crucial for business success but must be balanced with sound financial management. The good news is that today's landscape of AI and affordable marketing tools, empowers small businesses with the right knowledge and approach.

As outlined in the previous chapter, start-ups and smaller businesses will benefit from creating buzz and exploiting word of mouth marketing. Getting people to talk about you, your product or service or even your marketing all have a part to play in generating momentum. Whilst the effects of buzz are often short-lived, brands have to start somewhere. People love sharing news and information, and exploiting this is probably the most cost-effective form of advertising. So, find or create something about you that people can start talking about. Make full use of any customer/user-generated content you can and make sure your reviews and customer feedback are shared and clear for everyone to see.

Our research into brand growth revealed that certain media excel in building momentum. While TV emerged as a strong contender, brands recently seen on YouTube achieved an even higher index. This is fantastic news for start-ups, as it confirms access to affordable, highly targeted advertising that can drive momentum. The success of TV and YouTube underscores the power of video in generating momentum and the crucial element of emotion.

As we've discussed, altruism also drives momentum. Demonstrating a commitment to doing good – whether that's supporting your community, caring about something, or showing how your product improves lives. Many consumers are cynical about business owners, assuming a sole focus on profit. While this isn't always fair, overcoming that bias can be an uphill battle, hindering customer empathy towards small businesses.

One crucial image attribute driving momentum is vitality. Many start-ups naturally possess this due to their fresh energy, making them appear youthful, enthusiastic and exciting. This gives start-ups an advantage, hinting at potential popularity and success. So, maximise your vitality while you've got it!

Some companies mistakenly try to rush past the launch phase, downplaying their newness to emphasise trustworthiness and familiarity. This rarely works – skipping this step prevents you from capitalising on the energy of your introduction. Remember, a vibrant brand image is attractive and encourages people to buy now or keep you in mind for the future. So, make a splash, embrace your newness, and get excited! At some future point, you may even need to strategically re-inject vitality to keep your brand thriving.

Prospective buyers crave proof of a business's success and ability to deliver. Reviews, word of mouth recommendations, and industry awards all create a powerful impression. Testimonials from satisfied clients are among the most effective ways to provide this proof. Consider taking this further by seeking out local, niche, or national awards recognising your expertise – this can be especially valuable if you market to other businesses.

Conveying confidence and success is crucial when customers choose a provider. Any tangible evidence you can offer will be invaluable. While it's tempting to overstate your abilities, honesty with clients is the only sustainable approach. This includes transparent pricing, realistic timelines, and accurate website information. Even admitting mistakes or areas where your company is still developing can reinforce your strengths. Clients are more likely to trust you when you're forthright.

As a business owner, you'll quickly discover that no one will ever care about your business quite as much as you do. Overcoming this challenge is crucial. Hiring the right people is a crucial step, but fostering a culture of shared commitment and engagement is the key to true collaboration and business success.

In business, attention to detail is paramount. When seeking to build brand momentum, don't just focus on the big picture. Consider the impact of the little things—a specific word, a carefully chosen image, or a seemingly small action. Every detail sends a signal, and these signals often determine one brand's success over another.

Building momentum on a shoestring budget requires strategic thinking and relentless focus. While a comprehensive momentum strategy may feel out of reach for smaller businesses, the core principles explored in this chapter are absolutely transferable to your situation. Let's recap some key takeaways:

- Centre your business around understanding your customers' needs and how you provide solutions. Your goal isn't simply awareness; it's making customers care.
- Embrace the inherent vitality of being new – it attracts customers and signals potential success. Don't rush to shed your newness!
- Choose your words and visuals with intention, and never underestimate the importance of consistent details. This includes being honest with clients and promoting an engaged team culture.

Part 4 Round-up

Momentum is the secret ingredient for creating successful marketing. Brands with a high BVS have an undeniable buzz that fuels growth. The good news is you can strategically create momentum through thoughtful advertising and marketing.

Creativity truly sets campaigns apart. Deep audience insights fuel top-performing ads and give them that special something to make them memorable. Outspending competitors whenever possible also propels growth. For sustained momentum, focus on brand-building advertising alongside efforts to attract new customers. Think of a continuous drip campaign constantly reinforcing your brand's presence and velocity.

Momentum is the fuel that powers unstoppable brands. The keys to creating it are consistent brand-building advertising with a creative spark, a relentless focus on growth, and signalling success through thoughtful marketing choices. And remember, where you advertise and how you execute your marketing tell a story about your brand.

"Momentum is the fuel that powers unstoppable brands."

BRAND MOMENTUM: The #1 Growth Metric for Every Boardroom

A Final Word

Life is like riding a bicycle. To keep your balance, you must keep moving.

Albert Einstein

It has been six months since I first sat down to start writing this book, but I am pleased to say that Mack is still here by my side, curled up and sleeping, albeit with some heavy breathing and, dare I say, snoring!

began writing this book on a three-week holiday through the Greek Islands. With no prior writing experience, I quickly realised that completing it within three weeks was impossible – especially with limited internet access for the necessary research. However, the subject matter resonated with me, and the ideas flowed. What started out as a short 30-minute ebook has grown exponentially and become much more than I had hoped or ever anticipated.

Momentum is about a journey, and as the deadline for this book approached, I recognised the story was just beginning and would continue to evolve. If I wasn't careful, I'd never finish! Acknowledging its incompleteness and the need for further research, I knew publishing was the only way to generate interest and propel the narrative forward. And so I have come to the end, and my research and writing, for now, is done!

However, I believe there is still much to learn and do. We must understand what drives our notions of growing and declining brands and how marketers can amplify these factors. We are also developing a new approach to pretesting advertising and messaging to predict their ability to generate BVS and momentum.

To stay updated, please visit www.tonylewis.me for resources. We will launch an online training programme and workshops for those seeking more formal instruction, bringing the lessons from this book to life.

What will you do next? I hope you enjoyed this book, and would love to hear your ideas. Please share your thoughts, stories and challenges with me at www.linkedin.com/in/tonylewis1).

Good luck!

References

1   2023 CEO Survey — The Pause and Pivot Year, Gartner Research, 17 April 2023, https://www.gartner.com/en/documents/4277899

2   Article in MIT Sloan Management Review · June 2006

3   https://en.wikipedia.org/wiki/Benz_Patent-Motorwagen

4   https://www.experianplc.com/newsroom/press-releases/2023/half-of-all-new-businesses-fail-within-three-years-of-opening

5   https://www.coursehero.com/file/p6d4pdb3/Probably-the-most-famous-marketing-example-was-the-Mason-Haire-Nescafe-coffee/

6   https://en.wikipedia.org/wiki/List_of_cognitive_biases

7   Performance Brand Placebos: How Brands Improve Performance and Consumers Take the Credit. April 2016 Journal of Consumer Research 42(April):931-951. Authors Aaron Garvey, Frank Germann and Lisa E. Bolton.

8   https://en.wikipedia.org/wiki/Mere-exposure_effect

9   https://psychology.fandom.com/wiki/Mere-exposure_effect

10 https://www.linkedin.com/pulse/brand-purpose-moving-beyond-bullshit-nick-liddell/

11 https://www.pwc.com/us/en/services/consulting/library/consumer-intelligence-series/future-of-customer-experience.html

12 https://www.journalofadvertisingresearch.com/content/56/4/352

13 https://www.thinkbox.tv/news-and-opinion/newsroom/why-tv-remains-the-worlds-most-effective-advertising

14 https://vimeo.com/373969781

15 Mark Ritson's Effectiveness Top 10, https://thinktv.ca/wp-content/uploads/2019/11/ThinkTV-ritson_summary.pdf.

16 https://www.thinkbox.tv/research/thinkbox-research/the-drivers-of-profitability#the-drivers-of-profitability

17 What's working in growing market share| Article | WARC Category Intelligence | April 2024

18 Robert Brittain and Peter Field, 'To ESOV and Beyond', Advertising Council Australia, 2021.

19 https://www.thinkbox.tv/research/thinkbox-research/marketing-effectiveness-in-the-digital-era-media-in-focus

20 Binet, Les., Field, Peter. The Long and the Short of it: Balancing Short and Long-term Marketing Strategies. United Kingdom: Institute of Practitioners in Advertising, 2013.

21 https://www.yumpu.com/en/document/view/31998159/asi-admap-article-10-rules-for-tv-strategy-dec2014#google_vignette

22 https://www.warc.com/content/paywall/article/warc-exclusive/how-small-businesses-can-use-tv-advertising-to-grow/en-gb/127681?

23 https://www.thinkbox.tv/research/thinkbox-research/signalling-success

Bibliography

Part 1

Rowling, J.K. *Harry Potter and the Philosopher's Stone*. United Kingdom, Bloomsbury, 1997

Part 2

Cialdini, Robert B., and Cialdini, Robert B. *Influence: The Psychology of Persuasion*. United States, HarperCollins e-books, 2009.

Du Plessis, Erik. *The Branded Mind: What Neuroscience Really Tells Us About the Puzzle of the Brain and the Brand*. United Kingdom, Kogan Page, 2011.

Gladwell, Malcolm. *The Tipping Point: How Little Things Can Make a Big Difference*. United Kingdom, Little Brown Book Group, 2022.

Keller, Kevin Lane. *Strategic Brand Management: Building, Measuring and Managing Brand Equity*. United Kingdom, Prentice Hall, 1998.Larreche, J.C., The Momentum Effect: How to Ignite Exceptional Growth

Ries, Al, and Ries, Laura. *The 22 Immutable Laws of Branding*. United Kingdom, HarperCollinsBusiness, 2000.

Romaniuk, Jenni. *Building Distinctive Brand Assets*. Australia, Oxford University Press, 2018.

Romaniuk, Jenni. *Better Brand Health - Measures and Metrics a How Brands Grow World*. Australia, Oxford University Press, 2023.

Sharp, Byron. *How Brands Grow: What Marketers Don't Know*. Austria, OUP Australia & New Zealand, 2010.

Sharp, Byron. *How Brands Grow 2: Including Emerging Markets, Services, Durables, B2B and Luxury Brands*. United States, Oxford University Press, 2021.

Shotton, Richard. *The Choice Factory: 25 Behavioural Biases that Influence what We Buy*. United Kingdom, Harriman House, 2018.

Sutherland, Rory. *Alchemy: The Surprising Power of Ideas That Don't Make Sense*. United Kingdom, Ebury Publishing, 2019.

Thaler, Richard H., and Sunstein, Cass R. *Nudge: The Final Edition*. United Kingdom, Penguin Books Limited, 2012.

Part 3

Cialdini, Robert B., and Cialdini, Robert B. *Influence: The Psychology of Persuasion*. United States, HarperCollins e-books, 2009.

Gladwell, Malcolm. *Blink: The Power of Thinking Without Thinking*. Penguin, 2006

Kahneman, Daniel. *Thinking Fast and Slow*. Penguin, 2012

Larreche, Jean-Claude. *The Momentum Effect: How to Ignite Exceptional Growth*. Pearson Education, 2008.

Part 4

A Master Class in Brand Planning: The Timeless Works of Stephen King. Germany: Wiley, 2011.

Bartlett, Steven. *The Diary of a CEO: The 33 Laws of Business and Life*. Ebury Edge, 2023

Berger, Jonah. *Contagious: Why Things Catch On*. United Kingdom, Simon & Schuster 2014

Binet, Les, and Field, Peter. *Media in Focus: Marketing Effectiveness in the Digital Era*. Institute of Practitioners in Advertising, 2017

Binet, Les., Field, Peter. *The Long and the Short of it: Balancing Short and Long-term Marketing Strategies*. United Kingdom: Institute of Practitioners in Advertising, 2013.

Dweck, Carol. *Mindset: The New Psychology of Success*. Random House Publishing Group 2007

Sutherland, Rory. *Alchemy: The Surprising Power of Ideas That Don't Make Sense*. United Kingdom, Ebury Publishing, 2019.

Milton Keynes UK
Ingram Content Group UK Ltd.
UKHW020326190924
448477UK00004B/5